UFO's
WHAT ON EARTH
IS HAPPENING?

John Weldon
with
Zola Levitt

HARVEST HOUSE PUBLISHERS
IRVINE, CALIFORNIA 92707

Dedication

To the faculty and students of the Light and Power House, 1972-1975, with my deepest appreciation and gratitude.

Acknowledgments

I would like to express my sincere thanks to the following people for their kind assistance in various ways: Sharon Lindsley, Linda Kaeding and Beth Turner for their excellent typing on a manuscript requiring perseverence; Dr. James F. Coppedge, Professor Harold Slusher and Mark Arrington for help on some technical points, and Vicki Trembley for her kind general assistance. A very special thanks is due Bill Counts for selflessly offering his time, even with a very busy schedule. Without his concern and assistance, this book might not have been published. I would also like to thank Hal Lindsey and Walter Martin for reading the manuscript and offering their comments; Zola Levitt for re-writing the manuscript, and publisher Bob Hawkins for his continuing dedication and hard work.

The author extends his personal thanks to the following publishers for their kind permission to quote from the following copyrighted material. Thanks is also due to the NOAA Environmental Data Service and the World Data Center for Solar Terrestrial Physics for their information on earthquakes and sunspot frequency.

Doubleday and Company, Inc.
ALIENS FROM SPACE, copyright © 1973 by Donald E. Keyhoe pp. ix; 221; 17, 18, 157.
URI: A JOURNAL OF THE MYSTERY OF URI GELLER, by Andrija Puharich p. 88 (Bantam edition) © 1974 by Lab Nine Ltd.
Ballantine Books, a Division of Random House, Inc.
UFO'S: PAST PRESENT AND FUTURE, by Robert Emenegger, © 1974 by Sandler Films Inc. p. viii-ix.

Harcourt Brace Jovanovich, Inc.

FLYING SAUCERS, copyright, 1959, by Carl G. Jung pp. 116-117.

THIS VIEW OF LIFE, copyright, 1964, by George Gaylord Simpson, exerpts from "The Nonprevalence of Humanoids".

Henry Regnery Company

PASSPORT TO MAGONIA by Jacques Vallee © 1969 by Jacques Vallee pp. 110; 150; 40-41; 57; 158-59, 163.

THE HUMANOIDS by Charles Bowen, ed., © 1969 by Flying Saucer Ltd.

ANATOMY OF A PHENOMENON: UFO'S IN SPACE by Jacques Vallee © 1965. p. 138.

PSYCHIC MAGAZINE, 680 Beach St., San Francisco, Ca. 94109, "UFO's: The Psychic Component' by Jacques Vallee, p. 17.

FLYING SAUCER REVIEW (FSR), P.O. Box 25 Baŕnet, Herts, EN5 2NR, England

Bantam Books, Inc.

BEYOND EARTH: MAN'S CONTACT WITH UFO'S by Ralph Blum with Judy Blum, copyright © 1974 by Ralph Blum, p. 223.

Massachusetts Institute of Technology Press

COMMUNICATION WITH EXTRATERRESTRIAL INTELLIGENCE, by Carl Sagan, ed., © 1973, pp. 362-364.

Academic Press, Inc.

THE ORIGINS OF PREBIOLOGICAL SYSTEMS, copyright © 1965 by Academic Press, Sidney Fox, ed., exerpted from "The Folly of Probability" by Peter T. Mora.

Fawcett Publications, Inc.

OUR HAUNTED PLANET, copyright © 1971 by Fawcett Publications; by John A. Keel, p. 107.

Starmast Publications.

TO THE YOUTH OF THE WORLD, copyright © 1973 by The Universal Industrial Church of the New World Comforter, channeled through Allen-Michael.

Used by permission:

Lockman Foundation,

NEW AMERICAN STANDARD BIBLE, and NEW TESTAMENT, © 1960, 1962, 1963, 1968, 1971.

Contents

Chapter 1. What On Earth Is Happening?   3

*Birthpangs? . . . The Human Climate . . . Something
Is Up . . . Worldwide Sightings . . . Chariots of
Gods? . . . Identifying Flying Objects . . . The
Enemy Above . . . The Silencers . . . Power Black-
outs—On Schedule . . . Alone in Space? . . . A
Cover-Up? . . . Scientific Respectability . . . Ask the
Man Who Knows One . . . Skeptical Investigators
Convinced . . . Our Destiny—Decided Elsewhere?
. . . Aquarius And The Angel Of Light*

Chapter 2. Now You See 'Em Now You Don't   19

*A Plague of Flying Objects . . . Dramatically In-
creased Sightings . . . The Friendly Skies? . . . Get It
in Writing . . . Cover-Up in the Dark Ages . . . The
Age of Reason? . . . The Great God Man . . . You
Name It . . . From Fireballs to Jets . . . The "Good-
year Blimp" Period—And Beyond . . . Ghost Fliers
. . . Then the "Kraut Balls" . . . Enter Project
Grudge . . . Is The President at Home? . . . The
Cover-Up . . . The Today Show*

Chapter 3. UFO's—Do You Believe?   43

*Government Sits Up . . . Enter—The Antichrist? . . .
The Real Believers . . . "UFO on Our Tail" . . . Do
You Believe? . . . UFO of the Year . . . October 11,
1973 . . . The Hickson-Parker Case*

Chapter 4. And For Their Next Trick   57

*Help—If You're Up There . . . Worlds Unknown . . .
Exploding the "Big Bang" . . . Mystery Within a
Delimma . . . Evolution—Not Repeatable . . .
Don't Bet On It . . . All In The Family? . . . The Un-*

scientific Method . . . The Rules Don't Count . . . Now You See It – . . . Another Law

Chapter 5. The Bible and The Berkeley Messiah   73
The Bible Tells Us So . . . A Case in Point . . . Demon Talent . . . The Berkeley Messiah . . . Revelations Revealed? . . . Would You Believe? . . . A Dangerous Trip . . . Psychic or Psycho? . . . The Spirit of the Antichrist . . . Principalities and Powers

Chapter 6. The Occult Connection   91
The Duke Experiments . . . UFO's and the Occult . . . Getting in Touch . . . The Professor Speaks . . . Beware the Black Magic . . . Possession and the "Kindly Persuaders" . . . Because Their Deeds Are Evil . . . The MacKay Papers . . . Teletransport

Chapter 7. Testing The Spirits   109
The Only One to Save Mankind . . . Another Reality? . . . Spectra Calling . . . God Is an Idea . . . Dr. Puharich's Masterpiece . . . Hook or Hoax? . . . The Voice of Interplanetary Parliament . . . The Cosmic Masters . . . Another Gospel . . . The Parallel World . . . The Sinister Revival

Chapter 8. Let Us Take You To Our Leader   127
The Puzzles . . . Recapping the Evidence . . . Today's Sophisticate – An Occultist . . . The Answers . . . Who Turned Out the Lights? . . . Betty Hill's Stars . . . The Coming Invasion . . . Interstellar Apostasy . . . The Truth Will Set You Free . . . Receiving Christ

Appendix 1. Are the U.F.O. Occupants Good Beings?

Appendix 2. The Bible and Life in Outer Space

Appendix 3. The Popular Theory on U.F.O.'s: A Valid Option?

Appendix 4. Life by Chance in Outer Space: Possible or Impossible

Appendix 5. The Methods/Further occult correlation.

Introduction

Though most UFO sightings can be found to have a natural explanation, it is the growing conviction of scores of scientists and professionals worldwide that a very significant minority (from 20-30%) are truly unknown aerial phenomena. Most reports are never investigated so the exact percentage of truly unidentified objects is unknown. Even if all cases could be explained naturally, which they cannot, problems would still remain since the UFO phenomena consists of more than just sightings. There are over 2,000 cases of human encounters with landed UFO's and their occupants, and 700 cases of physical evidence left behind. There is also the issue of certain UFO close encounter effects in three distinct areas: 1) the electromagnetic effects in the mechanical, 2) the strange and often fearful reactions of animals, and 3) the physical and/or psychological effects upon humans. The apparent dangers of UFO research, the great number of varied occult connections, as well as the numerous contactee reports (Keel estimates 50,000 in the U.S. alone) cannot all be accounted for on the basis of naturalistic theories. The implication that UFO's (not necessarily flying saucers) are real seems more probable than having thousands of people all over this planet, down to the last one, reporting misidentifications of natural phenomena and perpetrating hoaxes. When so many "errors of observation" can produce an annotated bibliography of 400 pages, when increasing numbers of serious scientists the world over begin to believe in UFO's and when a $525,000 21 year official Air Force investigation fails to solve the problem, then it seems logical to assume we are dealing with a real phenomena. Thousands of people claim contact with extraterrestrials. A continuing worldwide debate and sociological phenomena does not arise from nothing.

The theory we now present to you is unusual in the least. But no more unusual than the UFO phenomena itself.

ABOUT THE AUTHORS

Zola Levitt, a Hebrew Christian, graduated from Duquesne and Indiana Universities in Music. He has a Ph.D. from Indiana, and has performed with the New Orleans Philharmonic, San Antonio Symphony Orchestras, and Glen Campbell Show tours. He is a marriage counselor and member-in-training for Psychoanalysis. Levitt met the Lord in 1971, and is now a Christian author, lecturer and radio talk show host. His best sellers, SATAN IN THE SANCTUARY, and THE COMING RUSSIAN INVASION OF ISRAEL, both written with Dr. Thomas S. Mc Call, and ISRAEL IN AGONY, are among his dozen books.

John Weldon received his B.A. degree with honors from California State University of San Diego in 1972. He graduated with distinction in Sociology. In 1975 he completed third year studies at The Light and Power House, a Biblical Training School in Westwood, California. He is a research editor for the Christian Research Institute. UFO'S: WHAT ON EARTH IS HAPPENING? culminates several hundred hours of inquiry about UFO'S, the occult and the evolutionary theory. The book is a significantly condensed and popularized portion of the larger manuscript.

New York City (New York). During the great power blackout, actor Stuart Whitman was startled to hear a whistling sound outside his 12th floor window and to observe two hovering objects, one orange and the other blue, giving off a luminescent light. He then heard an English message indicating that the blackout was a "demonstration". (Nov. 9, 1965, dawn.)

Jacques Vallee,
Passport To Magonia, # 715

From all indications, this [UFO controversy] is one of the greatest problems our world will ever have to face—even if no danger is ever involved.

Major Donald E. Keyhoe (Ret.)
Aliens From Space

Once exposed to the facts, even if you were a disbeliever, you cannot help but have new and probably different feelings about the subject. The evidence supporting the existence of this unexplainable phenomenon is overwhelming.

Robert Emenegger
UFO's Past Present and Future

There is no greater challenge to thinking people than the integration of UFO reality into the life on planet Earth.

Stanton Friedman (nuclear physicist)
MUFON 1974 UFO Symposium

Man sent out a powerful radio signal Saturday in an attempt to communicate with other civilizations in the universe. . . . The signal was beamed from the world's most powerful telescope . . . [and] was by far the most powerful ever beamed from earth . . . the equivalent of one million suns deep in space.

Los Angeles Times
Nov. 17, 1974

If these things are real—and by all human standards it hardly seems possible to doubt this any longer—then we are left with only two hypotheses: that of their *weightlessness* on the one hand, and of their *psychic nature* on the other. . . . Of course, next to nothing has been gained as regards the physical explanation of the phenomenon, but the psychic aspect plays so great a role that it cannot be left out of account.

Dr. Carl G. Jung
Flying Saucers

U.S. Scanning 3 Stars for Signals From Other Beings.
Los Angeles Times,
May 23, 1975.

What On Earth Is Happening?

The UFO's are real! Those "Unidentified Flying Objects" are really up there. Millions of people the world over have seen them, including unusually reliable observers of all kinds. Scientists, government leaders, the military, clergy, and ordinary citizens everywhere are seeing them regularly.

It's time to decide what they are and what they want.

Birthpangs?

Our age is very special. Never before have we known so much about ourselves and our world, and never before have we suffered so much for it. This is a frightening time. Political, economic, and military unheavals around the globe are daily occurrences. Famine is rampant in large parts of the world. Environmental deterioration threatens to alter our way of life permanently. Serious crimes are on the upsurge everywhere. Rich powers are stockpiling nuclear armaments, while poorer nations watch in dread.

We are seeing strange and threatening changes in our natural habitat. Even the weather is playing havoc with our world lately. Our planet is being increasingly ravaged by natural disasters: blizzards, tornadoes, hurricanes, floods, frosts, and drought have decimated food crops around the world and have left millions homeless and destitute. Undersea volcanic activity is on the rise.

Every year there is an average of 940 earthquakes measuring 5.0 or greater on the Richter scale. Tornadoes, readily counted, have shown a devastating increase, from 160 per year during the period 1924-49, to 624 per year during 1950-73.[1] The National Oceanic and Atmospheric Administration has stated that "drastic changes" in the climate around the world are now in progress. Some scientists are saying that the earth is going headlong toward a period of tremendous geological upheaval. It is possible that large amounts of magma (the earth's molten interior) are becoming increasingly active within the core of the planet.

Sunspots have increased in size and number, and the solar activity in general is beginning to worry some observers. The sun has emitted one hundred times the energy in radiation storms that we should expect relevant to its inner core structure. This worrisome activity is similar to the signs a star gives off before it "explodes" (or actually implodes).[2]

Jesus spoke of wars, famines, earthquakes, etc., and said that these were "birthpangs" (Matt.24). One is tempted to think of something very big indeed going on in connection with our recently increased geo-physical phenomena. Psychics everywhere proclaim that a great upheaval is due somewhere before the year two thousand.

The Human Climate

There are big changes in the climate of humanity, too. New advances in science and medicine have made these fields virtually inaccessible in their fullness even to the studied professional. In sociology and psychology ominous new horizons bode a new and strange impact on human existence as we know it. Occultism, mind control, legalized drug use, cybernetics, and behaviorism, to mention a few, present an inexplicable future for the customary norms of man's behavior. Social values and individual morality no longer find agreement even among the experts. New ways of behaving—utterly alien to all that has gone before—seem to be in the offing. People don't know what to believe in anymore.

Weird upheavals in the human climate have happened before in our history, and with dire results. Before the flood of Genesis 6, during the time of Christ, and in the incredible world of Hitler, something like "powers of darkness" showed themselves in obvious ways. Men were maddened and they perpetrated horrible atrocities in their madness.

Some theologians credit demons, like the ones mentioned throughout Scripture, with the periodic global manifestation of evil which have plagued our world. Lewis Sperry Chafer warns that, "A similar increase in the activity of demons is predicted for the close of this age and in the Great Tribulation."[3]

Something Is Up

We are not the first people in our world's history to see UFO's. Records of sightings exist from all periods, and we will give some of them below. But today the sightings are accelerating in number, with the last thirty years presenting a virtual explosion of this phenomenon. Something definitely is up, and it will be the purpose of this book to assign a cause and a reason for the UFO's.

We think demons are behind this startling phenomenon, and we think their activity is connected with the upcoming Tribulation period. As Christians, we believe that the Bible has demonstrated its accuracies in many ways. Viewed in this context, the activity of demons at this particular time is not at all surprising or strange. Indeed, it is to be expected, and, unfortunately, the worst is yet to come!

First, let's look into the actual recorded sightings of UFO's and the hair-raising encounters that result from their visits. We will cite reliable, available sources for our findings, and we will examine carefully all pertinent data. There are reasons why government and the media have not provided the whole story, but it is available and it is important.

We should endeavor to keep exceptionally open minds in order to pursue so strange a topic. Believers need have no fear of undertaking an investigation into demon activity, but others must be careful to keep a firm rein on their imaginations.

Christians and non-Christians alike should be concerned. Whatever your position might be in regard to supernatural phenomena, you have a right to raise questions and look for answers.

Worldwide Sightings

According to known reports UFO's are sighted around the world in the thousands. In the U.S. reports about sightings rarely hit the major papers. Yet just one U.S. UFO group, The Center for UFO Studies, generally receives several reports daily on their "hotline", open only to professional agencies (the F.B.I., police, etc.,) and *not* the general public.[4]

In any case, reported sightings occur everywhere with varying regularity. The United States, Russia, Brazil, France, and Africa have had numerous sightings; indeed, every nation seems to be included. Several years ago, Yugoslavs were reportedly "running in shock" to escape what they interpreted as an actual UFO invasion.[5]

The frequency, number, and nature of the reported incidents is fairly similar all over the world.[6] When an especially large number of sightings is reported in a short time, the phenomenon is referred to as a UFO "flap." In 1965 and 1967 there were large international flaps. The summer of 1972 and fall of 1973 saw our country experience a series of flaps. The later ones were much better covered in the news media, perhaps due to the preparation in progress of an NBC White Paper on the subject of UFO's.

The most startling report from the October flap was the temporary abduction of two Pascagoula, Mississippi, shipyard workers, who said they were taken aboard a UFO for twenty minutes and examined.[7] There are hundreds of similar reports.

UFO's seem to have become bolder recently. In the past twenty-five years they have been sighted over every major European and American city as well as over military installations and nuclear sites. The Soviet Union maintains a permanent UFO inquiry section within their reputable All-Union Cosmonautics Committee. As in the United States, the USSR has experienced a constant stream of reported sightings. According to prominent Soviet scientist Felix Zigel, there are well-documented reports of UFO's from "every corner of the USSR."[8]

Chariots of Gods?

A certain fascination with UFO's has been increasing steadily over the past few years. The three books of Eric von Daniken, author of the incredible *Chariot of the Gods?,* have sold over twenty-five million copies. The public seems almost "occult-hungry," and some of this interest has spilled over into the realm of UFO's in a big way.

Von Daniken's books, which speculate that the earth was visited by creatures from outer space thousands of years ago, have a fascination of their own, of course. But the interest in UFO's also stems from very objective sources. A Gallup Poll released November 29, 1973, indicated that some fifteen million adult Americans have personally seen UFO's!

A similar survey in 1966 indicated five and a half percent of the adult population had seen UFO's, so the sightings have about doubled in just seven years. In addition, the 1973 poll showed that fifty-one percent of those interviewed believe UFO's are real. Books about UFO's, once strictly a science-fiction buff's item, are being published and read widely by the general public.

Qualified scientists and some government personalities are becoming very interested in the UFO's despite the Condon Report, a two-year investigation which concluded that "further intensive study of UFO's probably cannot be justified in the expectation that science will be advanced thereby."

The Aerial Phenomena Research Organization (APRO), with representation from fifty countries and including thirty-eight consulting Ph.D.'s of various sciences, studies UFO's very seriously.

Recently, Sen. Barry Goldwater, a Major General in the Air

Force Reserve, took a position on the Board of Governors of the prestigious National Investigation Committee on Aerial Phenomenon (NICAP).

Astronaut James McDivitt, Dr. J. Allen Hynek, Chairman of the Department of Astronomy at Northwestern University, and Charles Hickson, one of the men who reportedly boarded the UFO at Pascagoula, appeared together November 2, 1973, on the Dick Cavett talkshow for a serious discussion of UFO's.

Identifying Flying Objects

The sightings of UFO's and the testimonies of those who say they have seen them operate at close range or have even been aboard them have contributed little to our understanding of them. People everywhere are still mystified as to what they are, where they're from, and what they want. Identifying these flying objects is extremely difficult.

The vast majority of ufologists believe the objects are actual physical craft from another world. A lesser group holds that, due to the strangely erratic behavior of the objects, they are from another dimension—a source simply unfathomable to us. They feel the craft are "semi-solid" or "semi-physical." A third group believes that at least some of the UFO's are of a spectral nature—having a ghost-like quality. The latter position is related to an incident occuring on October 1, 1948, when Air National Guard Lieutenant George F. Gorman reported that he had fought an air "duel" with a luminous, but apparently non-material, craft. Finally, we cite those who believe that the UFO's are creatures themselves, not machines. They think the craft we sight may be the outer shells of the creatures.

No one of these classifications fits all of the data we have amassed about UFO's, and some are, of course, unsatisfactory to those who wish to account for every natural phenomenon with a purely material explanation. But the enormous number of sightings and reports of actual contact leave those who do not admit to the reality of things spiritual in the untenable position of simply denying the existence of the UFO's. They have to keep saying that the sightings are all false or that common natural phenomena explain the "UFO's" adequately.

This is an imaginative exercise in itself. The more obvious physical phenomena that have been pressed into service to account for the UFO sightings are sometimes more far fetched than the UFO theories themselves.

The moon, temperature inversions, light refraction, migrating birds, clouds, mirages, stars, marsh gas, ball lighting: all have been utilized to explain various UFO sightings. It is also sometimes said that we haven't adequately explained all natural phenomena as yet, so that a UFO sighting can be chalked up to some inexplicable phenomenon of the skies. Most UFO's are, in fact, strange "blobs of light" in the sky.

Finally, the UFO's are inevitably characterized as some secret weapon of the enemy (American or Communist, depending upon which side of the Iron Curtain they were sighted).

It should be stated that most of the sightings do have a natural explanation, and some may be deliberate hoaxes. But the prevalence of their occurrence—everywhere, regardless of international boundaries and ideologies—begs the question. To imagine that extraterrestrial neighbors were paying a call would strain the credulity no more than to dismiss all the sightings as hoaxes or the result of natural phenomena.

The recent book *UFO's Past, Present and Future* discusses the many sightings from 1947-1973 with a good deal of cogent verification. Most of the cases cited are from the official files of the U.S. Air Force and are presented in cooperation with the Department of Defense and NASA. The author calls the evidence for the existence of UFO's "overwhelming." The book presents incidents of sighting UFO occupants and actual cases of contact. The material will present much food for thought to skeptics.[9]

The Enemy Above

Unfortunately the UFO's are no friends of ours. Occasionally it is suggested that if these are visitors from another planet, we might try to cultivate good relations with them. A great number of people believe that contact with an advanced civilization could help mankind solve its problems.

But what if they aren't friendly? Apart from the fact that some who claim contact with extraterrestrials cite positive relationships, there are other and more sobering reports to consider.

Bizarre and frightening incidents of which we can mention only a sampling here are recounted in connection with the UFO's. Were we to mention all of them, it would take many books of this size to make an adequate report.

First, it is apparent that those heavily involved in UFO investigation suffer a higher-than-normal death rate.[10] Then some of those who have pursued the UFO's in planes have come out very badly. Many pilots—some reports say fifty or more—have lost their lives in this way, and a few have suffered unprovoked attacks from UFO's. In one case, bodies with gaping wounds were recovered from an aircraft filled with a terrible, rotten stench.[11]

Mysterious noises, brilliant but inaudible explosions, and jets of flame have been associated with the UFO's. Equally dramatic are the "hypnotic rays" which have reportedly enveloped and stunned observers. Abductions have been cited on rare occasion, including sexual assault and rape, with both males and females involved.[12]

Offensive and frightening as they are, these reports have been culled from published data, presumably verified and accurate. As with all phenomena of the occult world, some may be exaggerated or fabricated. The vast numbers of reports and their similarity in widely varied circumstances, however, argue for their veracity. Our own hypothesis—that the UFO's represent demon activity—allows for the kinds of reports we are giving and the even more unsettling ones to follow.

That UFO's occasionally land on the ground is lent credence by the indentations that have been found at possible land sites. A strange residue may be left on the ground, later to vanish. In rare instances, cows and smaller animals have been found at these places—mutilated or cut completely in two.

Teleportations, the supernatural transporting of an individual over some distance, have also been associated with the UFO's.

John A. Keel, described as one of the foremost UFO investigators in the world, has reported a great increase in what he calls "phantom helicopters." According to Keel, these machines have appeared in some twenty states from New York to California.[13]

The Silencers

One of the most unusual and disturbing UFO-related phenomena are the appearances of the "men in black." Their mission, reportedly, is to destroy UFO evidence and frighten observers into silence. Though they seem to have stepped right out of a late movie on the horror show, their activity and appearance have repeatedly been a feature of UFO reports. John Keel reports a variation of these unsavory characters, which he calls "cadavers" because of their extreme thinness and their pale and bloodless appearance. Some twenty-five people have described these horrible thin men.[14]

Giants, ranging from ten to nineteen feet in height, have been reported in Brazil, Argentina, Australia, Spain and other countries. Government agencies have received reports of these beings using paralyzing rays, attempting kidnappings, and otherwise terrorizing observers.[15]

Mysterious disappearances of people and machines have also been reported during UFO flaps. Sometimes they reappear thousands of miles away, sometimes never at all. In some cases the people experience amnesia. Airplanes, ships, cars, and even trains have vanished. According to Keel, the disappearances are absolutely documented, no matter how hard they are to believe.[16] In one case, an observer who signed a notarized affidavit regarding the veracity of his story claimed he saw a bell-shaped UFO descend over a jet plane and simply take it up and haul it away. A jet was reported missing in that area that day, and it has not been found yet. In Brazil a man had his car pulled along by a "huge glowing ball" at a speed of 100 miles an hour for a distance of several miles. It was quite a performance for the low-powered car, according to the shaken driver.[17] Interestingly enough, the Bermuda Triangle, famous for its mysterious disappearances, also has a high number of reported UFO sightings.

Power Blackouts—On Schedule

It's quite possible that the enemy above was related to the four-state power blackout of June 5, 1967, and the large-area blackout of the Northeastern United States and Southeastern Canada on November 9, 1965. UFO's were reportedly seen near the high tension wires at Niagara Falls and in New York just prior to the 1965 event. A few weeks before the 1967 blackout occured, Ted Owens, a psychic and "contactee," wrote a letter to the *Saucer News*, stating that he would ask the extraterrestrials to cause this specific blackout. The idea, Owens said, was to bring attention to the upcoming UFO convention. The blackout came on schedule.[18]

Uri Geller, the Israeli psychic, says that he is in communication with "space intelligences," and that they have claimed responsibility for the blackout in Israel of January 14, 1972.[19]

Stories like those seem to establish the UFO's as part of an intelligent operation intended to harrass or disrupt the activities of this planet, if not to accomplish something more drastic still. And the evidence continues to mount. Some people have actually reported the existence of UFO bases on the earth. Some even claim to have been inside.[20]

Alone in Space?

Much effort today is going into finding out if we're alone in the sea of space or not. Incidental to those findings will be information about the possibility of the UFO's coming from intelligent life elsewhere in space.

Exobiology, a new science, is concerned with life beyond Planet Earth. In August 1975, NASA's billion-dollar Project Viking will launch two unmanned spacecraft equipped to search out life on the planet Mars, our near neighbor. Speaking of this fascinating probe, *Time* magazine remarked, "Should Viking find even the most primitive organism, it will help confirm what many scientists suspect: that life is not unique to the earth and is probably commonplace throughout the universe."[21]

In an effort to relate UFO's directly to life in outer space,

The National Enquirer offered a $50,000 reward to the first person to submit proof that UFO's are extraterrestrial. Entries have been submitted, but none has taken the prize as yet.

A Cover-Up?

Former astronaut Edgar Mitchell is understandably interested in exobiology. His institute for Noetic Sciences, a parapsychological research organization, has investigated the claims of Uri Geller, who freely admits to extraterrestrial contact.

Project Bluebook was the official designation for the U.S. Air Force high-security investigation into UFO's. (Project Sign, the initial study, and Project Grudge, which debunked the reports, were preceding investigations, 1947-1952). Bluebook went on for some twenty years, but eventually concluded that UFO's were not a national security risk and probably did not originate outside this planet.

Physicist Edward U. Condon was contracted by the Air Force from 1966 to 1968 to undertake a thorough investigation of the UFO's, but the Condon Committee report also came out negative, as we have seen.

In 1969, before the most recent flaps, Project Bluebook was officially closed. By 1970 several scientific organizations and responsible investigators had declared Condon's conclusions unacceptable.[22]

Scientific Respectability

Certain foundations continued the study of UFO's when the government appeared to abandon it. Research is being conducted by APRO and NICAP, and also by two newer groups, the Mutual UFO Network (MUFON) and the Center for UFO Studies. The latter group was founded by "convert" Dr. J. Allen Hynek, who had served as a learned skeptic on Project Bluebook A highly regarded astronomer, Dr. Hynek is attempting to lend UFO study some measure of scientific respectability. According to the *Los Angeles Times* of March 17, 1974, he claims the support of 500 to 600 professionals, including "numerous people at government labs."

All of the groups are international in scope and draw heavily upon the resources of the scientific community. Their major objective is to re-interest the government in this research and to reopen the UFO investigations with staff and funding commensurate with the gravity of the problem.

Project Cyclops is a different approach to the life-in-space question. Sponsored by Stanford University and NASA's Ames Research Center, Cyclops, if implemented, plans to build antennae capable of receiving electromagnetic waves from outer space and to "listen" for life. This is an especially fascinating approach because, as we will explain below, electromagnetic waves are tied to more than one system of reality.

The cost, unfortunately, is tremendous and the track record for this kind of research discouraging. An earlier attempt, Project Ozma in 1960, failed with lesser equipment and was criticized widely as a pipe dream.

Ask the Man Who Knows One

Nobody has ever been on another planet—or we should say, nobody from earth—but some people claim to have had "contact" of some kind with extraterrestrials. We have mentioned these "contactees" in passing, because they frequently associate themselves with UFO's, or those who "man" (?) UFO's.

It's often not appreciated just how many of these stories have been published in our times, or how frequently someone claims contact with non-earth spacemen. Naturally this takes place in some people with vivid or damaged imaginations, but again, the weight of the evidence favors belief in many of the stories. Some unquestionably reliable witnesses have been involved in this particular issue, as we shall show.

Since 1897 there have been at least 2,500 contact stories published around the world. Of course this just represents those who came forward, willing to be investigated, laughed at, and so forth.[23] We'll present such a story, with its source, before going on to discuss the contact question.

The incident actually took place in 1959, but the information was classified by the government until 1974, probably due to the involvement of government personnel of intregity and reliability and the extraordinary nature of the case.[24] Suppressing material of this nature—material so strange that it might have a panicking effect on the general public, is perhaps understandable.

Ths case involved a woman from Maine who claimed to be in contact with extraterrestrials, and she was able to give extraordinary data about the planets. She discussed outer space as if she were very familiar with its inhabitants and gave a cogent picture of extraterrestrial society. First the Canadian government investigated her claims extensively; then the United States government became interested.

Skeptical Investigators Convinced

Two U.S. Naval Intelligence officers were dispatched to interview the remarkable lady from Maine. They came equipped with questions about outer space and technicalities of the subject that would normally be well beyond the civilian grasp.

The woman went easily into a state of trance, in which she was able to supply the investigating officers with new information concerning a "Universal Association of Planets." This UAP was at work on its "Project Euenza" (Project Earth), she informed the officers.

The skeptical officers didn't know quite what to make of all of this, but they were *really* stunned when the woman indicated that the space beings would be just as glad to make contact with one of the officers! True enough, when one of the investigators volunteered he went into the trance state and immediately began giving additional UAP information. He apparently was receiving telepathic messages!

His associate questioned him closely about the sensations as well as the information he was receiving, and though he knew him well, he couldn't place anything the new contactee was saying. It was, to the best recollection of the questioner, new knowledge coming from his colleague.

And that wasn't nearly the end of it. The contactee officer was subsequently examined carefully by a group of CIA and military personnel. He went into the same trance before that group, and this time he offered proof of the contact with the extraterrestrial personalities. He said that if the group would go to the window, they would see a UFO before their eyes. They went as directed and—there it was! They *all* saw it.

Meanwhile, the woman from Maine identified the beings she was in contact with, along with their planetary addresses, as: Affa, from Uranus; Crill, from Jupiter; Ponnar and Alomar, from Mercury; and Ankar, from Centaurus.

Crill gratuitously supplied her with the population of Jupiter (787,730,016) and the information that the Jupiter day is seven times longer than the Earth day!

The whole matter, admittedly, sounds rather like science fiction, and the names (titles?) of the woman's planetary acquantances sound quite typical of that whole fairy-tale realm. But there's no getting away from the fact that the incident so impressed the government that it was suppressed, and no adequate alternate explanation has ever been given. We are dealing here with highly skeptical CIA and other Intelligence people who are used to scrutinizing evidence and personalities.

Our Destiny—Decided Elsewhere?

We might also assume that other material is being withheld. If this particular incident was acceptable for release, we wonder what might not be. Has contact been made with our leaders? Is our destiny already decided by aliens?

The idea of a UAP, or a United Planets Organization, is a rather common contactee revelation from the extraterrestrials. Their testimony is naturally suspect on many grounds, but the idea has also been considered by eminent scientists. Dr. Carl Sagan, Cornell University astrophysicist, speaks of a Central Galactic Information Repository. Dr. Fred Hoyle refers to an Interstellar "club." *Newsweek* remarked that a growing number of scientists believe in a United Interstellar Organization (like the U.N.). It has been suggested that Earth may one day be asked to join this United Planets Organization and that the extraterrestrials may be preparing us for this very event.[25]

One author believes that the UFO occupants are purposely leading the world into the "Age of Aquarius" through their mental and psychic powers. They intend to uplift the human race to make us worthy of a place at the United Worlds Council. He cites that under the UFO influence there has been a dramatic upsurge of interest in ESP and psychic phenomena. He feels this will signal the beginning of a Golden Age—one that will mark a higher spiritual level for all mankind.[26]

Aquarius And The Angel Of Light

This mind-boggling idea—that the human race is about to enter some new, more spiritual kind of existence—is really not out of line with Bible prophecy. Many feel that the signs of the end times given by Jesus are well-matched with the natural and spiritual phenomena of this age, and that our times qualify as the "end times" in prophecy.

The end times, in turn, mark the return of Jesus Christ and the setting up of His Kingdom on the earth—truly a golden age and a higher spiritual level—but only for redeemed mankind.

There's a big problem with equating the Kingdom of Christ and the Age of Aquarius. The latter is a man-made, occult-centered, rather naive way of looking upon the manifestations of our times. The Age of Aquarius concept is an application of sorts of the "power of positive thinking" to what is in reality deadly evil. What may appear to be new gains in man's knowledge and understanding, amounts in reality to a deadly decline into the Tribulation. That Garden tree, whose violation ushered in Sin and Death, was called the Tree of Knowledge.

The devil, the Scriptures warn, poses effectively as an Angel of Light. He provides intellectual knowledge and a positive attitude to deluded men, and he accomplishes his ends while they rest in a false confidence. Those who look upon such phenomena as the UFO's, contactees, and the occult as benevolent are playing into his hands.

We rather think, as we have said, that the UFO's and the other strange manifestations we are seeing represent demon activity, and we will show our reasons later on. Suffice it to say now, that anyone would be well advised to tread lightly in these areas. Fascination with the occult has been with us for a very long time. Perhaps the UFO's have also been around long before this present age of "enlightenment." We will examine that. But bear in mind that we are opening areas of inquiry that are fraught with dangers of a kind few are accustomed to handling.

Believers should approach these phenomena prayerfully, aware that we are privileged to understand easily what is a befuddling mystery to the rest of the world. Our God has instructed us in the realities of demon activity. We read of our Lord confronting these powers fearlessly and defeating them. We realize that "the battle is the Lord's." We reach only for a greater understanding of this world and the one to come.

The author's wish for all men is only for safety and deliverance from what is going on. Only through an accurate knowledge of what we are seeing today can you combat this ingenious approach of the devil. Only through understanding what is being done with our human race at this time can you effectively avoid the terrible consequences to come.

The Bible is very clear on the phenomena we are experiencing in the world today, and very clear, as well, on the way of escape from their dire results. If you are without the Biblical knowledge to comprehend this, we will explain it all below. We ask only for open minds and a little tolerance of our time-honored but much criticized viewpoint—sometimes called the "oldtime religion."

Can oldtime religion make any headway against a brand-new phenomena that man has seemingly never confronted before? Can Christian soldiers still go onward in the face of startling new developments that mystify scientists and stun high government officials? Are we who offer the maligned Gospel of Jesus Christ of any use today? We think so. Read on.

FOOTNOTES

1. *The World Almanac,* 1975 (New York, Cleveland: Newspaper Enterprise Association), p.816; cf. *Science News,* Jan. 25, 1975, p. 52; Otto O. Binder, *Saga's UFO Report,* vol.1, no. 6.

2. Walter R. Martin, as interviewed by *Right On*, Sept. 1973 (P.O. Box 4307, Berkeley, California 94704), p. 11.

3. Lewis S. Chafer, *Systematic Theology* (Dallas: Seminary Press, 1971), vol. 2, p. 117.

4. *Saga's UFO Special*, vol. 3, p. 4, 29; *Nature*, Oct. 4, 1975, p. 369; Center for UFO Studies Bulletins, Jan-May, 1975 (P.O. Box II, Northfield, Illinois, 60093);

5. Glen McWane and David Graham, *The New UFO Sightings* (New York: Warner, 1974), p. 147.

6. Ralph Blum, *Beyond Earth: Man's Contact with UFO's* (New York: Bantam, 1974), pp. 181.

7. Ibid., chaps. 1-3, 12, 17. See also *Bulletin of the Aerial Phenomena Research Organization, Inc.* (Tucson, Arizona 85712), Sept–Oct. 1973.

8. Blum, *Beyond Earth*, p. 189.

9. Robert Emenegger, *UFO's Past, Present & Future* (New York: Ballantine, 1974), pp. viii-ix, 55-73.

10. John A. Keel, *Our Haunted Planet* (Connecticut: Fawcett, 1971), pp. 92, 113, 128.

11. Ibid., pp. 206-8. See also D. Keyhoe, *Aliens From Space* (New York: Signet, 1973), pp. 157-175.

12. Ibid., pp. 160-61; Charles Bowen (ed.), *The Humanoids* (Chicago: Henry Regenery Co., 1969), pp. 200-239; and Jacques Vallee, *Passport To Magonia* (Chicago: Henry Regenery Co., 1969) pp. 116-29.

13. McWane, *The New UFO Sightings*, p. 32; Max Flindt and Otto Binder, *Mankind: Child of The Stars* (Connecticut: Fawcett, 1974), p. 238; the *1974 Mutual UFO Network Symposium*, p. 86 for Keel recommendations.

14. McWane, p. 28; Keel, pp. 103-116; Brad Steiger *Flying Saucer Invasion* (New York: Award 1969) pp. 117-126 for men-in-black information.

15. C. Bowen, *The Humanoids* (Chicago: Henry Regenery Co., 1969), pp. 84. 102-107, 151, etc., *Saga's UFO Special*, no. 3, p. 20.

16. John A. Keel, *Our Haunted Planet*, ch. 15. See also Keel, *Saga's UFO Special*, vol. 3, p. 13.

17. *Saga's UFO Special*, 1973, p. 6.

18. McWane, p. 111; Blum, pp. 118-9, 156; Donald E. Keyhoe, *Aliens From Space* (New York: Signet, 1973), pp. 176-186, 222; *Facts on File: A World News Digest with Index.*

19. Dr. Andrija Puharich, *Uri* (New York: Bantam, 1975), p. 160.

20. McWane, p. 27.

21. *Time*, Sept. 2, 1974.

22. Blum, pp. 169-170; *Saga's UFO Special*, vol. 3, p. 4; Brad Steiger, *Flying Saucer Invasion:* "A Criticism of the Condon Report" by John A. Keel.

23. John A. Keel, *Saga's UFO Report*, Spring 1974, pp. 8, 37.

24. Emenegger, *UFO's*, pp. 55-62.

25. Otto O. Binder, *Saga's 1973 UFO Special*, pp. 38-39, 42; Flint and Binder, p. 243; Blum, p. 210.

26. Otto O. Binder and Canadian Scientist Wilbert B. Smith, *Saga's 1973 UFO Special*, p. 46.

The most appealing of the theories proposed, which would regard the UFO's as probes from another planet, falls short of explaining the phenomena in their historical development. Present-day saucers cannot be evaluated without references to the 1897 airship or to earlier sightings of similar objects.

Jacques Vallee
Passport to Magonia

Anyone who would understand history must be in possession of the category of the demonic.

Helmut Thielicke

Among the omissions were the transocean crash and the Braniff 1959 disaster; the AF attempt to down a UFO near Redmond, Oregon, proved by FAA logs and traffic controllers' reports; the 1958 AF transport encounter, where the captain reported they were "shot at" by a UFO; and other serious and significant cases. Cases of UFO-caused injuries were left out or denied, including airliner near-collisions in which passengers were hurt.

Major Donald Keyhoe
referring to the
Condon Report in *Aliens From Space*

For the time being, the only positive statement we can make, wihout fear of contradiction is that it is possible to make large sections of any population believe in the existence of supernatural races, in the possibility of flying machines, in the plurality of inhabited worlds, by exposing them to a few carefully engineered scenes the details of which are adapted to the culture and superstitions of a particular time and place.

Jacques Vallee
Passport to Magonia

The real UFO story must encompass all of the many manifestations observed. It is a story of ghosts and phantoms and strange mental aberrations; of an invisible world which surrounds us and occasionally engulfs us; of prophets and prophecies, and gods and demons. It is a world of illusion and hallucination where the unreal seems very real, and where reality itself is distorted by strange forces which can seemingly manipulate space, time, and physical matter—forces which are almost entirely beyond our powers of comprehension.

John A. Keel
UFO's Operation Trojan Horse, Ch. 2

2

Now You See 'Em
Now You Don't

UFO's seem to have been around for a long time. We can find odd references to "circles of fire in the sky" in many historical documents and even in cave paintings. While we seem to be experiencing a great upsurge in reported sightings in our own day, every age seems to have had similar stories.

Occasionally new sightings persuade previous UFO observers to lose their reticence in telling all. As UFO's become a more acceptable topic of interest, many observers come forward with stories they'd hesitated to divulge before. Of course a lot of people just want to get on the bandwagon—perhaps in some sectors of occult studies a sighting would qualify as a religious revelation—but again, reliable observers are found.

A Plague of Flying Objects

Both United Press International and Associated Press quoted U.S. Air Force Chief of Staff General George S. Brown on October 18, 1973, as he recollected UFO activity during the Vietnam conflict. He stated that unidentified flying objects "plagued" the United States during that war and even started an air-sea battle in which an Australian destroyer was hit. He said the UFO's were "atmospherics," not space craft.[1]

People came forward to cite UFO action in World War II as well, bringing up the interesting but frightening idea that the enemy above has been with us for a longer time than we'd like to think about.

There's some evidence for that.

If one holds to a purely materialistic theory about the UFO's—that they are a weapon of an opposing earthly civilization—the idea of visitations in the distant past is unacceptable. But both the visitors-from-space theory or the demon theory easily allow this. The Scriptures refer to activity of a demon kind as far back as the Garden, of course, and scientifically speaking, if we are being observed by a far superior extra-terrestrial civilization, it would likely have been very interested in our past development. We were probably an interesting species to watch, as we continued our technological advances, and the heightened interest in us now, evidenced by the increased number of recent sightings, may reflect a curiosity as to how we are going to finish ourselves off. If we were a good show with the blade and the torch, we must be fascinating with the bomb and the missile!

Actually, the Biblical teaching of demon activity coincides with our penchant for self-destruction; Satan's war with God over which way men will turn (Job, e.g.) could be won through racial suicide. But prophecy indicates that God is aware of those possibilities, and the Second Coming of Christ (in the nick of time) will avert complete disaster: "Unless the Lord had shortened those days, no life would have been saved," reads Mark 13:20. God's attitude is clear: "[The Lord is] patient toward you, not wishing for any to perish" (2 Peter 3:9).

In any case, whatever theory is held about the UFO's, there is evidence that they have been here before—a long time before—and this adds a new perspective to their activity.

Dramatically Increased Sightings

The number of recorded observations for all time up to 1954 was around 10,000.[2] Since then, there has been a dramatic upswing of sightings into the millions. Either people are becoming less reticent to talk about this increasingly familiar phenomenon, or the UFO's are actually here in much greater numbers today. Possibly the UFO's *want* more people to believe in them at this point. If so, their public relations campaign has been very effective—and upsetting.

Again, we must say that not all sightings are necessarily genuine, and the ones of the past are even more suspect. We can only offer the evidence and sources for consideration. We can only say that men noted strange objects in the skies and left evidence of their observations as far back allegedly as 45,000 B.C.

The Friendly Skies?

Accurate dating methods before about 10,000 B.C. are open to question, we must first say. Physical chemist Dr. Melvin Cook of the University of Utah says there really are no reliable longterm radiological "clocks," and even radiocarbon time measurement is in serious need of repair.[3] From a scientific standpoint we have some difficulty in saying how old the earth is, and the idea of billions, or even millions, of years of development has been challenged by competent scientists. Keeping that in mind, we proceed to look at the UFO-related evidence of the distant past.

Granite carvings in a mountain cave in China's Hunan Province show figures with large torsos standing upon cylinder-shaped objects in the sky. Below them, pictured on the ground in the carvings, are other similar figures (the artists?). These carvings have been dated at 45,000 B.C.

Some seventy-two caves throughout France and Spain show drawings dating from around 13,000 B.C. of a variety of oval and disc-shaped objects resembling at least the shapes of today's UFO's. Researcher Ralph Blum, recipient of Fullbright, Ford and National Science Foundation grants, says in his book *Beyond Earth: Man's Contact With UFO's* that the caves seem to comprise a virtual "catalogue" of modern UFO designs. He also notes that the religious books, legends, and histories of many diverse cultures of ancient times describe beings coming down from the skies.

The Bible does the same in Genesis 6, where the "sons of God" held a high appreciation for mortal women:

> Now it came about, when men began to multiply on the
> face of the land, and daughters were born by them, that
> the sons of God saw that the daughters of men were
> beautiful; and they took wives for themselves, whomever
> they chose (Genesis 6:1, 2).

God took a dim view of those goings-on:

> Then the Lord said, "My Spirit shall not strive with man
> forever, because he also is flesh. . . ." (Genesis 6:3).

The strange narrative, seeming to describe supernatural days
of cohabitation between the earthly and unearthly beings, continues with commentary:

> The Nephilim (giants) were on the earth in those days,
> and also afterward, when the sons of God came in to the
> daughters of men, and they bore children to them.
> Those were the mighty men who were of old, men of
> renown.
> Then the Lord saw that the wickedness of man was
> great on the earth, and that every intent of the thoughts
> of his heart was only evil continually (Genesis 6:4, 5).

Not all "sons of God" are positive spirits, obviously, and the
generally accepted theological interpretation of this passage is
that the "sons" are the angels who rebelled against God. Christ
referred to them as unclean spirits and demons. As such, their
coming down from the sky to intermingle with men is reasonable in the Biblical orientation. The devil himself is spoken of as
a heavenly rebel, deriving his supernatural powers from his
original position as one of God's angels. Is it surprising, then,
many civilizations noted in their literature and artifacts the
presence of supernatural beings, usually emanating from the
skies?

It is significant to Bible scholars that God's solution to the
dilemma of Genesis 6 was the Flood. Worldwide catastrophe
was the only answer to such prevalent wickedness as obtained
on the earth, a wickedness which didn't stop at accepting
demons as marriage partners. Now that humanity once more
finds itself caught up in a state of seeming global curruption,
worldwide tribulation looms on the horizon. In some sectors,
we see the ready acceptance of supernatural creatures again, as
in the contactee cases.

It is perfectly reasonable, from a Biblical point of view, to expect that the UFO's represent demon activity. Contact with them will grieve God, as it did in Genesis 6, and He will remonstrate with man in a disastrous way.

Get It in Writing

The literature of many cultures attests to sightings of odd celestial objects, and these references lead right up to the present. Apparently man has been spotting something like modern UFO's throughout all of his history and occasionally putting the matter in writing.

The early Hindu literature pre-dates the Christian era by about a thousand years. It contains references to "celestial and aerial cars," some of which are described as "a bright cloud in the sky." Some of the instances are strikingly reminiscent of our modern sightings. The epic poem "Mahabharata" refers to a blazing, spinning missile which radiates light and a tremendous heat. The "Samarangana Sutradhara" speaks of flying disc-like objects with exceptional maneuverability.[4]

Some ancient Tibetan books contain references to glowing flying objects that were used by persons of special religious status.[5]

While the above reports may be mythological, some of them, at least, might be valid descriptions of UFO's.

The Egyptians, no mean scientists for those early times also noted UFO phenomena. A papyrus record of the annals of Pharoah Thutmos III (c. 1600 B.C.) mentions circles of fire in the sky. The circles were as bright as the sun, according to the record, very numerous and dominating the sky. A terrible stench, a factor common to many modern reports, was associated with the appearance of these fiery disks.[6]

The writings of certain Roman historians, well corroborated in other areas, record incidents of unidentified objects in the skies over Rome in the third and fourth centuries B.C.[7] Wilkins specifies that Pliny, Seneca, Tacitus, and Lycosthenes, among several other reliable chroniclers of the time, all make mention of this phenomenon. Titus Livius and Julius Obsequens list eight specific locations of sightings, extending from the Gulf of shield" that swept across the sky, and the historian Livy used the words "phantom ships" when referring to celestial craft sighted in his time (60-17 B.C.).

There are very few reports of sightings in the first 500 years of the Christian era. Following the first coming of Jesus Christ, the UFO activity seems to have abated until the Dark Ages, or at least the written records bear little mention of it.

"Cloudships" and "Luminous Strangers" start popping up again in about the sixth century A.D. Glowing aerial objects become evident again in the literature of many countries. Jacques Bergier says that practically every year of the Dark Ages saw reports of "luminous strangers" being made.[8] Today, many people report seeing 'luminous beings' near landed UFO's.

Cover-Up in the Dark Ages

In 583 A.D. Gregory of Tours, the first historian of France, mentioned globes of fire that moved about in the sky.[9] Two hundred years later, during the reign of Charlemagne, four people were nearly stoned to death because they were seen falling (floating?) from "aerial ships." They were accused of sorcery, a capital crime. Their judges may have made an accurate charge: the defendants claimed they had been carried away by supernatural beings who showed them strange and unknown marvels and bade them to return and report what they saw. Agobard, the Bishop of Lyons, managed to have their lives spared by declaring that the event never really happened. Shades of Project Grudge![10]

In the Orient, a General Yoritsume spent the long night of September 24, 1235, with his Japanese troops, watching strange lights swinging, circling, and moving in loops about the sky until dawn. The General's investigation yielded one of those "natural phenomenon" results: he declared that the wind had caused the stars to sway.[11]

Fire during UFO sightings was not an uncommon occurrence in the reports. Wilkins records "wyld fire" from the skies that killed people and cattle, burned barns, and poisoned the grass during the years 1032, 1048, 1067, and 1694.[12]

In 1209 the monks of the Byland Abbey reported a large

round silvery disc that flew slowly over them and caused great terror, interrupting an otherwise quiet routine. The brothers of the Cistercian Abbey of Begeland were favored with two such visitations that year. Monastic records often mention UFO phenomena reported by shaken clerics. The thirteenth century was rather a vintage period for UFO's in England, with a large ship and fiery globe among the objects being sighted in the 1250's.[13]

On August 13, 1491, Facius Cardan reported an encounter with seven "men" who suddenly appeared to him. They claimed to be made of air, denied the immortality of the soul, and also denied that God had made the world for all eternity. They seemed interested in theological matters, and they described a system wherein God is constantly recreating the world, which would instantaneously cease to exist the moment it incurred God's displeasure.[14]

The Age of Reason?

With the coming of the Renaissance, man began to think more rationally and less spiritually, unfortunately. Art and science made great strides as men began to explore their world. Superstition of any sort had a very bad press.

Nevertheless, the UFO's kept on coming and increasingly so. No less a world traveler than Christopher Columbus reported one on October 11, 1492, just four hours before land was first sighted. He was walking the deck of the Santa Maria with a Pedro Gutierrez when the two saw a glimmering light moving up and down in the distant sky. Several times throughout the night it vanished and reappeared. No satisfactory explanation of the mystery has ever been offered.[15]

Columbus' explorations present an interesting exercise in thinking about UFO's and contact cases. From the Indians' point of view, Columbus was a creature from a UFO, borne to their shores by an Unidentified *Floating* Object, we might say. To those good builders of bark canoes, the explorer's ocean-worthy vessels must have seemed like much-advanced, supernatural craft indeed. Columbus took back some Indians to Queen Isabella, we know, and we assume that these first New

World tourists to Europe were received with great interest. But imagine *their* feelings! Wouldn't they have thought of this whole trip in the same way that the UFO contactees report their visits aboard mysterious craft or their contact with the extraterrestrials manning them? The Indians must have been thunderstruck at the "supernatural" appearance of the Spanish court and the incredibly advanced society which surrounded it. "There is no new thing under the sun" (Ecc. 1:9).

In the centuries following the Spanish explorations, other well-known people reported an increasing number of sightings. Worth noting are reports of astronomers equipped with optical devices of varied sophistication. In 1757 a British astronomer reported erratically moving celestial objects which changed colors as they crossed the sky and sped off at an impossible angle of flight. Two Swiss astronomers, working independently at Basel and Sole respectively, spotted the same large, spindle-shaped object with a radiant outer loop on August 9, 1792.[16]

The famed German poet Johann Wolfgang von Goethe, fearful of believing his own experience, wasn't certain if he had really seen "a company of luminous creatures" in the year 1768. But "luminous humanoids" also appeared to the California Indians in the 1700's. Their legend says that these beings had the ability to paralyze the Indians with a small tube.[17] Interestingly enough, a sort of paralysis gun was recently invented by John Cover. His "taser gun" sends an alternating current through the body, temporarily freezing the skeletal muscles.[18]

The German astronomer Kepler spoke of a benevolent demon who transported Kepler to the moon to help him with his research![19] This explanation rather went along with the popular idea of a good "muse" which would attend the efforts of poets, composers, playwrights, etc., often described as a "visitor" or "genius". The latter idea wasn't an attempt to describe anything occult (though some were), but in the case of Kepler's imaginings (?) we have something today's worshippers of the occult would well understand.

We will see in our chapter on demons that their supposed benevolence always has a price, as did the serpent's original offer of knowledge in the Garden.

The Mormon founders, Joseph Smith and Brigham Young, both thought the moon was inhabited. Smith apparently believed human beings lived there. Young thought the sun was inhabited as well! Mormonism in general believes in an infinite number of inhabited worlds.

We might scoff at the idea of the moon being inhabited, since we *have* been there and we didn't see any life. But in the world of demons, we suggest, life exists where it cannot be detected by our world. This is not so strange an idea as it may seem at first glance; religious people the world over, Christian and otherwise, have always believed in invisible beings. The living Jesus Christ, on whom so many base their faith, cannot be perceived by living human beings or their scientific instruments. He said, "Blessed are they who did not see and yet believed" (John 20:29) The issue seems to rest on just what sort of undetectable being we are willing to follow.

The Great God *Man*

The nineteenth century promulgated a view of man wherein he stood as the center of the universe. Men became "the measure of all things," and a phenomenal number of new "isms" and religious cults came forth. Scholars invented new ways of looking at things. Darwin's evolutionary theory, Kierkegaard's existentialism, Marx's *Communist Manifesto*, and Nietzsche's Superman theories gained popular acclaim. Cults of religion that sought to improve Christianity or make it more palatable rose out of the original. Spiritualism, Mormonism, Christian Science, Jehovah's Witnesses, and many other cults gathered followers.

UFO sightings increased considerably in this period. It would be quite difficult to try to draw a connection there, except to say that demon activity is a supernaturally planned total effort to oppose God. If the UFO's represent actual demon activity, they came to the right place at the right time in the nineteenth century!

The impressive list of philosophies and religions that came to the fore in that century might be called an advancement of intellectualism, but they might also be grouped under a decline of spiritual values. All of them are earth-centered, man-centered, do-it-yourself philosophies meant to replace the Christian ethic, and our world today is a direct result of their efforts.

You Name It

The UFO's increased their prevalence and variety steadily throughout the century, reportedly appearing almost everywhere in the western world and in every form imaginable. The various reported phenomena now included flashing lights, hovering objects, formations of UFO's, torpedo shapes, luminous aircraft, shiny discs, discs of various colors, circular objects with curved tails, impressive spiraling maneuvers, sometimes night-after-night appearances of the same phenomena and flight patterns, and on and on.

This varied display has continued to the present day. No two UFO's seem to be exactly alike. Certain phenomena do repeat, as we have seen, but there is no exact likeness, such as between two conventional aircraft, for instance. It's as if no one manufacturer makes all of them, or even as if they each have a different manufacturer. The saucer or disc themes definitely repeat more than others, but here again there always seems to be some basic difference in all sightings.

Among the hundreds of photos of UFO's and the many thousands of reported sightings, one baffling fact remains: they're virtually all different! The theory of visits from outer space suffers at this point, because we would surely expect the craft to be similar if they came from a manufacturing civilization. If we're having visitors from various civilizations out there, we've certainly attracted a mixture of them!

"Flocks" or at least very large numbers of UFO's flying together, were noted on two occasions in the nineteenth century. An 1849 astronomer's report described "thousands" of glowing objects moving across the sky.[20] On August 12, 1883, the first known UFO photograph was taken by José Bonilla, a Mexican astronomer associated with the Zatecas Observatory. Bonilla had been observing the sun when he suddenly saw an army of objects crossing its front. He counted nearly 150 of them, both cigar and spindle shaped and all visible in the photo.[21]

From Fireballs to Jets

An occult overtone of the UFO's is that their characteristics seem to match up with the particular civilization spotting them. That is, the Egyptians saw suns and the Romans fireballs; both were within their powers of description. Before the Machine Age arrived, the UFO's remained as "natural" phenomenon, describable without recourse to mechanical terms. But with the advent of the industrial revolution, the sightings were of flying "machines" rather than "luminous clouds" or "balls of fire". Nowadays we're seeking sleek jet-aircraft and rocket types of UFO's, quite in keeping with how we might design one ourselves. And we experience "non-material" craft, something within our imaginations but ahead of our technology. It appears that the "show" has always been uniquely adapted for its audience; or, to be more accurate, the show is always a little advanced and a little beyond the capabilities of the audience. The Romans weren't talking about the wide variety of craft that we see today. What they saw, instead, was close enough to the realities of their age to make them believe, but far enough beyond to leave them bewildered.

A good example of this was the sightings of the "airships" of 1896-97.[22] They seemed like something out of Jules Verne's science fiction, with their "propellors," porthole windows along the bottom, antennae, and submarine-like appearance. They had sharply pointed nose cones at the front and all sorts of streamlined appendages. There were dozens or perhaps hundreds of sightings of those ships. There was even a photograph, taken April 11, 1897, and pronounced genuine by the *New York Herald* and the *Chicago Tribune,* independently.

These rather cumbersome UFO's resembled designs already in the minds of some earthly inventors. C.A. Smith and H. Heintz took out patents on such ships in 1896 and 1897, respectively, but of course they never did succeed in building them. Six years later the Wright brothers flew their first heavier-than-air craft.

The "Goodyear Blimp" Period—And Beyond

This "Goodyear Blimp" period of UFO's seemed well-suited to the imaginations of its times and stimulated much wonder.

The craft were far enough beyond the capabilities of turn-of-the-century technology to discourage any thought of our going after them, but not so far beyond that they left the observers unable to describe them.

It's rather like a teasing game. When we advance, they advance. They're always a step ahead of us. Today they resemble the best of our aircraft in performance but far outdo our machines. Pursuit is hopeless, with the craft attaining to speeds and maneuverability well beyond our capabilities.

This whole idea—that the UFO's adapt to our culture—is suggestive that the whole thing is human imagination. After all, what the human conceives is always tied to his culture and surroundings. Jules Verne was able to dream up a credible electric submarine, but atomic power was simply beyond his grasp. And so the people saw airships, something already talked about in their culture. Maybe it was just their imaginations playing tricks on them?

Again, however, we're stuck with those multiple sightings and, at this point, even some photographs. Some very prominent people spotted the airships, but within a year or so the stories stopped coming in. Presumably the UFO's had come out with a new model.

A further documentation of the airships was the rather frightening abduction of a cow witnessed by farmer Alexander Hamilton in 1897.[23] Hamilton and two others saw an airship hovering thirty feet over Hamilton's herd and then hoisting a cow up to the ship by cable. Hamilton said he spotted six occupants of the craft, presumably through the portholes. The ship left with the cow, but next morning the head, hide, and legs were found in a neighboring field. Hamilton, a former member of the House of Representatives and considered a very responsible citizen, signed a sworn statement attesting to the incident. It was printed in the Yates Center *Farmers Advocate* of April 23, 1897.

Hamilton states that he was hit by a light beam from the airship just before it hoisted the cow, and this paralleled the "ray gun" phenomenon reported elsewhere. Hamilton apparently experienced no ill effects, apart from nightmares.

The airships had their contactees, if we are to believe the story of Frank Nichols,[24] who said he was taken aboard one of them. The "crew" explained the workings of the ship to Nichols, who understandably failed to comprehend the confusing lecture.

The airships were not nearly so reclusive as today's UFO's, cruising in a leisurely manner over large population centers such as San Francisco and Chicago. At that time we had no way at all of pursuit, so we couldn't determine the exact nature of these craft.

By the end of the 1800's, some people were accepting the idea of UFO's, though no one had the slightest idea of what they were or what they wanted. The total reported loss seemed to be one cow, but the enigma remained to trouble mankind as it entered the highly technological 20th century.

Ghost Fliers

Big flaps occurred in 1909 and 1913, with scores of new sightings in many countries. The UFO's were "improved" but still looked enough like blimps so that Germany felt she must publicly deny that her new dirigibles were involved.

Toronto, Canada experienced a fleet on February 10, 1913. England, Wales and Germany also reported sightings. Because the UFO's traveled very slowly, within reported ranges of twenty-five to one hundred miles per hour, they were observed carefully.[25] These wartime reports may be a little suspect, of course, since the presence of man-made flying objects was a new phenomenon to the public. Scares about superior air weapons were always prevalent, admittedly causing some imaginations to travel.

The period of peace between the world wars brought no letup. For months in 1933 Norway and Sweden were favored with nightly flocks of UFO's. The people called the unidentified airplanes "ghost fliers", and their constant comings and goings were routine. The frustrated Swedish air force tried to pursue the craft in December 1933, but the weather was miserable and cost the Swedes two planes. The planes were definitely lost to the weather conditions rather than by attack of the UFO's, some of the planes being unable to get airborne at all because of the storms.

The "ghost fliers" skillfully negotiated the stormy, mountainous regions, flying low and in formation, while the excellent Swedish pilots, experienced in the fine points of navigating the territory, had all they could do to stay in the air!

Though the "ghost fliers" were rarely seen to touch down anywhere, they were observed in close enough detail to determine that one of their craft had six engines and that none of them bore any insignia. They disappeared eventually and never returned. No evidence of any motive behind the flights was ever found.

Then the "Kraut Balls"

The Swedes got something of a break during the Second World War, during which allied pilots were harrassed by "balls of fire" flying in formation and by some very strange aircraft of amazing speed and maneuverability. These "foo fighters", or "Kraut balls", as they were dubbed, would hover at the wingtips of our fastest pursuit planes or fly in parallel formation with them. They seemed to have the ability to change shape in flight, as though they were made of flexible material. There were hundreds of sightings by pilots over three continents.[26]

Sweden was again subjected to UFO overflights right after the war, but now they enjoyed a newer model. The new UFO's were cigar-shaped rockets and faster than their forerunners, achieving a speed of five hundred miles per hour. The "ghost rockets", appearing by the thousands in the Scandinavian skies in 1946, emitted orange flames from their tails, suggesting rocket-type propulsion. They kept to low altitudes of one to three thousand feet, with apparently no fear of the forbidding mountains or the dangerous weather.

The Swedish military had received over six hundred reports by July of 1946, or about one hundred per month, and declared the situation "extremely serious." One month later sightings were reported in Finland, Spain, Greece, Portugal, and Turkey.

In the summer of 1947 these new craft apparently crossed the Atlantic in force, but now they were discs and saucers rather than cigar shapes. It was then that the term "flying saucers" came into vogue, though that term had to be extended because of later changes in the craft. Our present term, "Unidentified

Flying Objects," rather reflects how flexible we must be even to name these things!

Nineteen forty-seven was a vintage year and the start of the modern era in UFO-watching. During that year UFO's were seen wholesale in this country by trained observers and every sort of civilian witness. Our "visitors" were making themselves extremely obvious and a bit of a nuisance.

Enter Project Grudge

In April of 1947 the meteorology staff of a Virginia weather bureau was tracking a balloon when they spotted a silvery saucer-shaped object with a dome on the top. The experienced sky-watchers observed the UFO for fifteen seconds before it disappeared.

During the rest of the year sightings were legion throughout the United States, involving forty-six states and both military and civilian reporters. On June 21, when private pilot Ken Arnold saw a formation of nine saucers, the incident hit 150 newspapers. On June 28 a UFO chose to do some remarkable aerial acrobatics directly over Maxwell Air Force Base in Alabama. The following day Dr. C. J. Zohn saw one over the White Sands Proving Grounds in New Mexico. Additional sightings involved other strategic installations, including the Fairfield-Suisun Air Force Base in California and the Muroc Air Base (now the Edwards Air Force Base.)[27]

The U.S. Air Technical Intelligence Center at once became extremely interested in the UFO's! The Air Intelligence people conducted a preliminary investigation and concluded that the UFO's were real.[28] The recommendation of the investigators was for a high security study with a code name. The UFO's were going to undergo the most minute scrutiny, while the public was to be left out until something more definite was known.

Then, on January 7, 1948, Air National Guard Pilot Thomas Mantell lost his life pursuing a UFO. It didn't seem the UFO's fault. Mantell had just pursued the object to the unwise altitude of twenty thousand feet with an inadequate oxygen supply. Fifteen days after his plane crashed Project Sign was put into effect.[29]

The Air Force was charged with completely investigating the mystery of the UFO's. Project Sign eventually reported their reality and estimated them to be interplanetary craft. This report went all the way to the Air Force Chief of Staff, General Hoyt S. Vandenberg.

Vandenberg didn't like the whole idea, and there was a resulting stir in the ranks of Project Sign. They finally decided to offer a more innocuous explanation for the disturbing visitations. It was apparently concluded that all the sightings would be explained away as natural or psychological phenomena. Thus, in February of 1949, Project Grudge replaced Project Sign.

Many people were dissatisfied with Project Grudge and its explanations for the sightings. One who particularly had a grudge against Grudge was ex-Marine Major Donald Keyhoe. He published his own findings in December 1949 in a smasher of an article in *True Magazine* called "The Flying Saucers are Real." The media picked up on this sensational and well-researched revelation and gave it national coverage.

Oblivious, the Air Force published its *Grudge Report* during the same month, announcing an end to the project and the saucers. They had more or less explained away about three-fourths of the best 237 sightings.[30]

The UFO's must have felt slighted by the Grudge attitude, because they really outdid themselves in their next performance. The sightings had become only occasional, it seemed, but did include one radar tracking of five craft, one of them achieving Mach-plus speed at ninety-three thousand feet! Project Bluebook was undertaken to collect more data.

Then came the masterpiece! The UFO's decided to buzz the White House!

Is The President at Home?

It happened in the summer of 1952 and was truly a one-of-a-kind occasion, even for UFO's. The restricted air zone around the White House is one of the best defended areas in the world. Crack veteran jet aces stand by at all times with the finest of our interceptors at the ready. So—when the UFO's appeared in force, the jets were scrambled immediately. A true UFO chase was underway!

The jets didn't have a chance. (We can't use the expression "didn't have a prayer," because a prayer might have done the job, but more on that later.) When the jets came screaming into the White House airspace, the UFO's left the scene at better than seven thousand miles per hour. We didn't have a plane that could even keep them in sight. The base radar operators, following the whole operation clearly on their screens, were astounded. Having lost their prey, the jets were called home and the shaken pilots debriefed.

But suddenly the Alert sounded again! The UFO's were back. Again the jets scrambled and gave chase, and again the UFO's did their disappearing act!

This very upsetting hide-and-seek game went on for six hours at the pleasure of the UFO's, who almost seemed to be sporting with our aircraft. Finally, just before daybreak, the game was over. The UFO's called it quits and the weary pilots went off duty, completely mystified.

Things were quiet for a few nights while the radar people sat on the edges of their chairs. Then, the following weekend, at 3:00 A.M., the visitors wanted to play some more. Our security had to oblige. This time six to twelve UFO's appeared in two separate groups. Two F-94's were scrambled to meet them, one per group. The first pilot encountered them immediately, transmitting that he was closing on giant "blue-white lights" directly ahead of his plane. Then the lights surrounded him and it looked as if the chase were going to go the other way.

The pilot remained calm and transmitted that the lights were encircling his plane and closing in. Then, in almost a whimper, he asked, "What shall I do?"

The UFO's only observed the plane, without doing any kind of hostile action. In fifteen seconds they were gone, careening away at their usual stunning speed.

The pilots returned and the radar screens observed the UFO's for two more hours. Finally the visitors called it a night, to general relief.[31]

The rest of 1952 contained more and more sightings, and Project Bluebook, still trying valiantly to explain away the incidents, was kept very busy. The White House encounters were dismissed as "unusual atmospheric effects" or "optical and radar illusions," explanations that understandably left a host of questions still unanswered. In fact, the sightings continued reliably through the fifties.

A high point worth mentioning involved the White Sands Proving Grounds, our atomic testing field in New Mexico. Security there is severe, as befits the activities going on behind the fences. But in 1956 a domed, circular UFO paid a call about ten miles from the base and this one landed on the ground!

Havoc ensued. When the UFO touched down, close to busy U.S. Highway 70, nearby autos experienced electrical failures. Commuter traffic to Holloman Air Force Base, at the site of the proving grounds, began to back up. The situation thus created assured that everyone on the road clearly saw the landed UFO. Dozens witnessed to it, including two Air Force colonels and two sergeants.

The UFO remained stationary for some ten minutes. Then, with a whirring sound, it just took off and flew away without fanfare. All of this in plain sight of a highway full of observers.

This time the government agencies seemed to take the matter seriously. Though the Pentagon and the CIA joined the Air Technical Intelligence in investigating the matter, there just wasn't anything to report. No one had, or has to this day, the vaguest explanation for what they'd seen that day on busy Highway 70.[32]

The Cover-Up

The government started to think seriously in terms of a public panic, and they initiated what appears to be a deliberate cover-up. While the sightings have increased into the millions, and large numbers of UFO study groups have sprung up in this country and abroad, the official government position has been that the UFO's simply aren't there. The various government agencies may have, however, done the best they could in investigating UFO's. As we will see later, UFO's have a distinctly occult nature. Due to this psychic aspect, it would have been nearly impossible to find any real solution to the phenomena.

Some answer had to be found, however, for this was their job. It seemed that fear of public panic demanded a tranquilizer. Thus, UFO's became simply "natural phenomena", or even non-existent.

The CIA commissioned the Robertson Panel in 1953 to investigate whether the UFO's posed a true defense and security problem for the United States. The Panel responded, after their study, with the idea that the UFO's were not a real security problem, but that the continued reporting of sightings would not be beneficial to the country. Recommendations were made to remove the then-existing "special status" of the UFO's. The Panel reportedly recommended the "debunking" of the saucer reports and a general lessening of public interest in the subject.

Rather serious repressive measures followed the report. Within a few months Air Force Regulation 200-2 became operative, calling for an effort to reduce to a minimum the stories about UFO's. Then came Regulation JANAP-146, which made it a criminal offense for any military personnel to release information on "unidentifieds". Violaters could be liable to a fine of $10,000 and up to ten years in prison. In 1966 this Regulation was amended (becoming Regulation JANAP-146E) to include the processing of *non-military* reports as well as military ones. So, penalties apparently are still possible for the release of UFO information, military or civilian.

The Condon Report of 1966-68, which we have already cited, was another study which denied the danger and even the validity of UFO's. It is most interesting that this report was originally initiated after incumbent Congressman Gerald Ford had submitted a letter of concern about the problem of UFO's on March 28, 1966.[33]

There was reason for concern at the time. We have already considered the blackouts of August and November 1965 and the reported appearances of UFO's over Niagara, Manhattan, and Syracuse. UFO's were making the headlines at the beginning of 1966 as well, with concern mounting in high places.

However, the report again sought to disclaim, rather than really examine, the UFO's. The problem was that it brought up more questions than it answered.[34] The 1400-page Condon Report is in itself a rather valuable catalog of sightings, including a UFO that came within twenty feet of one observer, and a number of sightings by astronauts involved in several space trips. Most startling was the report of a UFO the size of the *Queen Mary,* with smaller discs coming and going from the craft! This UFO "base" caused quite a stir, and jets were scrambled; but it managed to vanish like its less formidable counterparts when the planes arrived.

The Today Show

The most recent developments in the UFO situation are shrouded in a veil of mystery, as we might well imagine. In the next chapter we will try to bring this matter up-to-date within the limits of what we are able to glean from various reports.

From the thousands of years of sightings, going back to the millennium before Christ, we have learned very little. About all we can say for sure is that the UFO's seem to have been around for a very long time and that they have changed with the times—or rather, a little in advance of the times.

From ancient times to the late nineteenth century, they were balls of fire or related configurations. Suddenly they became airships. Then, in this century, they became ghost aircraft and then ghost rockets. Now they have attained to an infinite variety of shapes and sizes, at the same time becoming much more blatant in their appearances. It seems they now routinely visit security sites, examine our sensitive depots of weaponry testing, and even drop in on the home of our President.

They remain impervious to encounter, except as they may choose, and the few stories of actual contact, whether physical or via spiritualistic media, are fascinating but hardly illuminating. We just can't seem to put a reasonable story together.

As matters stand, the UFO's go where they please and when they please. They violate anybody's airspace at will, and they are pursued only at the peril of the pursuer. They fly faster and higher and more expertly than any man can fly, and they touch down either with or without notice as they choose. They have largely spurned any communication of an official kind, and they have never made clear why they are here at all. Their attitude has seemed hostile in some cases, innocuous in most others. That they really are here seems now beyond any reasonable doubt.

But we just don't know what in the world they want.

FOOTNOTES

1. Blum, p. 177. I am indebted to the Blums for their concise history.

2. Aime Michel, *The Truth About Flying Saucers* (New York: Pyramid, 1974), p. 239.

3. Melvin A. Cook, *Prehistory and Earth Models* (London: Max Parish & Co., 1966); Walter Lammerts, ed., *Scientific Studies in Special Creation* (Presbyterian and Reformed, 1971), pp. 72-102; W. Lammerts, ed., *Why Not Creation?* (Michigan: Baker, 1970), pp. 80-114; H.S. Slusher, *Critique of Radiometric Dating,* (San Diego: Institute for Creation Research, 1973).

4. Howard V. Chambers, *UFO's For The Millions* (Los Angeles: Sherbourne), p. 37; A.C.B. Prabhupada, *Easy Journey to Other Planets* (New York: Collier, 1972); Louis Renow (ed.) *Hinduism* (New York; Simon & Schuster, 1971) pp. 119-133. Note: Many of these "UFO's" could easily be mythological; however, the Samarangana Sutradhara is reportedly a factual account, though a later (11th *C*) document.

5. Chambers, p. 37.

6. Harold T. Wilkins, *Flying Saucers Uncensored* (New York: Pyramid, 1974), pp. 77-78.

7. Ibid., pp. 7, 164; Michel, p. 239; Blum, p. 41.

8. Jacques Bergier, *Extraterrestrial Visitations from Prehistoric Times to The Present* (New York: Signet, 1974), p. 89.

9. Michel, p. 32.

10. Jacques Vallee, *Passport To Magonia* (Chicago: Henry Regenery, 1969), p. 5.

11. Blum, p. 42.

12. Wilkins, p. 76 and elsewhere.

13. Chambers, p. 38; Wilkins, pp. 70-71 for this paragraph.

14. Bergier, pp. 86-87.

15. Blum, p. 44.

16. Chambers, pp. 38-39.

17. Blum, pp. 44, 180.

18. Ibid.

19. Bergier, p. 91

20. Chambers, p. 43

21. Blum, p. 45.

22. Blum, ch. 5; McWane, p. 95. I am indebted to Ralph and Judy Blum for their historical survey, 1897-1968, from which most of this material is taken.

23. Blum, pp. 50-51.

24. Ibid., p. 55.

25. Jerome Clark, "The Phantom Airships of 1913," *Saga's UFO Report,* Summer 1974, p. 36.

26. See also Renato Vesco, *Intercept UFO* (New York: Grove, 1974), pp. 82-84.

27. Blum, pp. 73-6.
28. Ibid., p. 80.
29. Most material on projects Sign, Grudge, and Bluebook are from Blum, pp. 75-95.
30. Ibid; pp. 91-92.
31. Ibid., pp. 93-95; Emenegger, pp. 42-46.
32. Blum, p. 102.
33. Emenegger, pp. 73-6.
34. Blum, pp. 155-157, 162-163, 166; Keyhoe, pp. 206-223.

The official admission that UFO's are alien space-craft will startle millions and probably frighten many at first. But once the citizens know all the facts—and the lack of proven hostility—the hysteria should diminish. . . . Behind the scenes, highly placed secrecy opponents are working for a completely new, unbiased and open investigation of all the evaded and hidden evidence. It will probably lead to a full-scale crash program like the Manhattan Project, which produced the A-bomb, with thousands of scientists and engineers searching for clues to the UFO's advanced technology.

To reduce the chance of panic, officials would first release harmless reports from the thousands on record. The disturbing cases would probably be made public one or two at a time, the least startling ones at the beginning. . . .

Major Donald Keyhoe
Aliens from Space

Frankly, it is my opinion that the [U.S.] government is preparing us for some momentous news concerning UFO's—I detect some very clever groundwork being done and the sooner they tell us the truth, the better off we'll be.

Martin M. Singer, Editorial Director
Sagas UFO Report
Spring 1974

Observations similar to the landing at Pascagoula have been made every year in the United States since 1947. A computer catalogue of close encounter cases that I have compiled for purposes of content analysis holds the details of nearly two thousand cases of that type, from all countries, indicating that a formidable impact is being made on our collective psyche.

Jacques Vallee
Psychic Magazine
Feb. 1974

The F.B.I. has recently expressed its desire to cooperate with the Center for UFO Studies in helping to solve the UFO mystery.

April, 1975
New Bulletin from the Center

3

UFO's—Do You Believe?

December 15, 1974, was a landmark in UFO history. On that day the United States government may have started to bring the UFO's out of the closet.

The occasion was an NBC-TV Special entitled "UFO's—Do You Believe?" It was a fine beginning, very fair and balanced, if a bit conservative. The Special didn't say, "They're up there, folks; what do we do now?" But it did present some highly persuasive sightings, and the commentary was along the lines of "Here are the facts—decide for yourself."

The Special was made at least partly in cooperation with the Department of Defense. It appears to be the start of a several-year program which will gradually release information making it evident that the UFO's are real.[1] Ralph Blum has stated, "the most intriguing rumor around is that the Pentagon is covertly supporting a series of films for TV that will tell us UFO's are real". The idea is to uncover the story bit-by-bit, both to avert any possible panic and to avoid the feeling of a "great unveiling" of a government cover-up. Since Watergate, the American people don't like being taken for fools. They'd rather bear with the straight story, however disconcerting it may be, and that's what they're getting little by little.

The French government has come out with a more open attitude toward the UFO mystery, and there has been no panic in that country. In fact, Robert Galley, French Minister of Defense, has stated publically that the number of reliable UFO landing-occupant reports in his country is "very great" and "quite disturbing".[1a] With the United States government also owning up other countries may follow. The world may begin to take the visitors seriously.

Government Sits Up

According to one tabloid, both President Ford and Vice-President Rockefeller believe the UFO's are real and want more thorough investigations.[2] In any case, the declassifying of Defense Department material on the phenomenon is accelerating.

There won't be a breakthrough of information; the shock of "An Official Government Announcement" is obviously being avoided. Large numbers of people panicked back in the thirties when the Orson Welles program about a science-fiction invasion from Mars was broadcast, and the powers that be certainly want to avoid that, especially when the matter is not fiction!

Other government officials in addition to those in the White House have indicated an interest in the UFO's. We have already mentioned Senator Goldwater's affiliation with NICAP, a civilian UFO study group. There also seems to be some serious interest on the parts of Sens. Birch Bayh and Vance Hartke of Indiana and of Sen. J. Glenn Beall of Maryland. And, of course, with the government at large charged with the business of the welfare of the nation, there *should* be some concern about aliens of any sort in our airspace, not to mention their contact with our citizens.

The government will watch the public reaction carefully as the TV Specials go on. More T.V. films are scheduled for the future, including possibly a two-hour Special narrated by public protector figure Jack Webb (of "Dragnet").[3] If the public receives the new information without undue panic, the program of exposure will move into new phases. If, however, there is too much "scare" dialogue in reaction to the Specials, the "uncovering" will probably be discontinued and the government will go back to stonewalling it.

Considering all that was revealed in the initial Special by way of solid sighting cases and reliable witness testimonies, we shudder to think of what's coming up. Will this lead to contact with the UFO operators? Has contact already been made?

Or, for a real mind-boggler, have the UFO operators directed the government to have the Specials? Is this new government position part of the UFO public relations program?

That, of course, is mere speculation at this point, but again, in our demon theory contact is not only possible but certainly expected. The operators of the UFO's, as we see it, have come *expressly* to contact human beings. More on that below.

Enter—The Antichrist?

The most frightening possibility of all, from the point of view of Biblical prophecy, is that *somebody* will step out of a UFO with solutions to our world problems. A leading social psychologist feels that many people would actually welcome a humanoid being from another planet and might even set him up as a messiah or religious leader.[4] If this much-advanced fellow had some ideas to solve the evils of this planet, he would likely achieve instant popularity. It has been suggested already that an alien or a superior race might effect world peace where we have failed. This superior alien, with technological knowledge beyond our grasp, could effect what we might regard as miracles.

Don't put this book down yet. We may be about to meet the Antichrist!

The TV Special had become necessary because of all the "authority" sightings of the past few years. Back in the forties and fifties we had only a few military and "trustworthy individual" reports, but more lately these have become the rule. At a certain point, the government will either have to come clean or appear vastly behind the times.

Any number of public personalities have seen UFO's, from Senator Goldwater to Muhammad Ali.[5] The champ says he has seen UFO's on seven occasions, and nobody wants to fight him about it. More seriously, when people who have the public eye and ear begin to testify, the government simply must act.

Comedian Arthur Godfrey thinks UFO's are serious business since he almost collided with one in his plane some ten years ago. TV actor Roy Thinnes saw a UFO and became inspired to play the role of David Vincent in "The Invaders," a show dealing with extraterrestrial invaders. Jackie Gleason, who has a serious interest in occult and psychic phenomena, has seen two UFO's and is convinced that life exists on other planets. Sammy Davis Jr., Rolling Stone guitarist Mick Taylor, and many other well-known personalities have reported sightings.

In a rather unique story of UFO benevolence, William Shatner, the TV actor who plays the captain of the "starship" *Enterprise* on the serial "Star Trek," got highway directions from a UFO. Shatner got lost in the desert on a trip and spotted a UFO above. A voice from the visitor "impressed itself" on Shatner's mind, telling him the right direction to travel to safety. The actor believes the UFO saved his life and is grateful to his "fellow space travelers."

The Real Believers

One of the most convincing categories of sightings of recent years has been the experiences of the astronauts.[6] These real-life space travelers, hand-picked for their intelligence, calm, and technological expertise, can hardly be defamed as sensationalists. The articulate James McDivitt of the Gemini IV Crew was featured on the TV Special and testified to sighting a UFO.

McDivitt saw a cylindrical UFO with antennae which, for a moment, was on a collision course with the Gemini craft. The UFO pulled out of the course and McDivitt lost sight of it, but he saw three other UFO's during his mission. In each case the Ground Control unit experienced a blackout, somewhat hampering the monitering of Gemini. This is a common UFO-related phenomenon and suggests that the alien craft utilize jamming devices when they wish to avoid detection.

Gemini V experienced just the opposite situation. Astronauts Cooper and Conrad saw nothing, but Ground Control picked up the radar image of a tumbling object alongside the spacecraft and following its course. When the switch to the next radar tracking station came up, the tumbling object was no longer to be seen. Gemini VII astronauts Borman and Lovell also reported a tumbling object which they could not identify.

"UFO on Our Tail"

Then there was the rather hair-raising encounter experienced on the very first Gemini series flight, when Astronauts Grissom and Young were outright followed by four UFO craft who stayed with the spacecraft until it achieved orbit and then tracked it for one full orbit around the earth. The UFO's then "streaked off."

That story seems to underline the superiority of the UFO craft. What was a superlative effort by man—the achievement of escape velocity and an earth orbit—seemed to be a rather routine tracking exercise for the UFO. The alien craft apparently followed Gemini III only long enough to see what it was up to, and then appeared to lose interest. It makes one think of an adult looking in on children at play.

Gemini X was favored with a fine demonstration of formation space flying by the UFO's. Astronauts Young and Collins observed five UFO's traveling together in an earth orbit. A second report cited "two bright objects" that "just disappeared." The following morning another UFO appeared to the astronauts.

Two crew members of Apollo XI, Armstrong and Collins, described an L-shaped UFO "tumbling" in space.

Radio interference was caused when Apollo XII, with Conrad, Gordon, and Bean aboard, was tailed by two UFO's.

Skylab II had a leisurely visit from a UFO which was visible for ten minutes. It rotated slowly at about thirty to fifty nautical miles from the Skylab craft and was brighter than a planet or star. All attempts to identify it failed.

With all these NASA sightings now available, we must stress that there may be still more information classified. These are only the stories that were released, and then they weren't exactly put on billboards. Knowing the propensity and the good reasons for the government agencies to hold back on the more explosive dramas of this situation, we can wonder what remains untold. Did Apollo XIII, which we rescued from space damaged, experience hostile action from a UFO? How about the Russian flights that failed? Have we ever armed a space flight? Again, these are mere speculations. We look for more of the truth to come forward under the present government program.

NASA's position on UFO's is not really known, but the agency is very interested in the possibilities of extraterrestrial life. Various fly-by Pioneer missions are planned for the future, and they will carry life-detecting gear to our planetary neighbors within the solar system. In 1983 low-altitude probes of Venus will be undertaken, and in 1989 a landing on Venus may be tried.[7]

It is interesting that NASA has briefed its astronauts on how to respond if extraterrestrial life is encountered in space.[8] An exploration agency like NASA must, of course, leave no stone unturned, but we wonder how seriously the possibility has been considered that we have *already* encountered alien life, not only in space, but on the earth. We say "alien life" and not "extraterrestrial life" in keeping with our idea that the UFO's may represent life that is neither earthly *nor* extraterrestrial. Demons, in effect, do not have an address at all.

Do You Believe?

Getting back to the TV Special, we should review what was revealed in the light of the fact that it may be the start of a government turnaround. What we are being told is only what this government wishes us to know, if indeed the Defense Department is involved at a level some people seem to think. Our help may be solicited, or the government may have the very appropriate attitude that the UFO's *are* our business and we have a right to know what's happening.

The show began with sightings reported by ordinary citizens—small-town "heartland" Americans who have see UFO's. They spoke plainly, and there was little feeling of censorship in those stories.

Then the civilian agencies studying UFO's were given neutral coverage. The efforts of APRO, NICAP and MUFON, all of whom we have cited here, were examined, with brief explanations by the leaders of each organization. There was no atmosphere of ridicule apparent, and each researcher had his say in full. The skepticism of the researchers themselves was reviewed, and the fact that people try to foist phony reports on the agencies was brought out.

We were taken on a typical case investigation with one of the agencies and had the good fortune to be let in on an interview with an individual who had experienced a rather harrowing sighting. We saw several dogs at the scene, owned by the man who was being interviewed, and we were told that the dogs reacted far out of character when the UFO landed. The dogs apparently cowered in silence, not at all their normal reaction to strangers. The testifier was visibly shaken in recalling the incident.

Photos were screened by the dozen showing UFO's, or what appeared to be UFO's. It was explained that some were good fakes; others, it was stressed, had never been shown to be fakes. We were also shown the 5½ filing cabinets of sightings stored at Maxwell Air Force Base, involving 12,618 individual reports. According to Dr. Hynek, at least 23% remain unidentified.

UFO of the Year

Particularly persuasive reports were given by a U.S. Army helicopter crew, whose testimony won a $5,000 prize given by the *National Enquirer* for being the best UFO sighting report of the year. The entire crew, seasoned veterans of sky-watching and level-headed, plain-spoken soldiers, had seen a UFO on October 18, 1973, over Cleveland, Ohio. Their stories matched perfectly and no one has been able to discredit them.

A Boston policeman gave his sighting, with a feisty challenge to anyone to disprove it. He appeared in uniform and spoke decisively about what he had seen.

Motion pictures of apparent UFO's in flight were shown. The narrator said about one particularly convincing film, "Some say it shows two silvery, saucer-shaped craft; others say it shows the sun reflecting off two Air Force jets circling for a landing at a nearby airbase."

UFO detractor Dr. Carl Sagan also appeared, with commentary. He is an almost passionate opponent of the extraterrestrial theory and holds that the UFO's are not there at all. Two nights before the Special was aired he had told Johnny Carson on the Tonight Show," "There's as much evidence for flying saucers as there is for leprechauns."

His style was much more subdued on the Special, however. He said he wished for more scientific investigation of the phenomena and he called the existing evidence weak. He spoke of a meteor which had been seen by crowds of people, photographed, and perfectly documented, and he asked why this hadn't been done as conclusively in so many years of UFO study. He asked why, even if there *were* some flying objects we couldn't identify, people suspect visits from outer space. The conservative Dr. Sagan's comments follow, just as expressed on the program:

> There is, I suppose, a *tiny* but non-zero chance, that someday some spacecraft will appear in our skies from somewhere else, and that will, of course, be quite an extraordinary moment. But the fact that it's so important and so interesting shouldn't make us accept shoddy evidence. In fact, where we have an emotional, vested interest, we are required to be scrupulously honest—to demand the most rigorous tests; whereas in a problem where we don't have a big emotional stake, we would be happy to accept evidence that's not quite as rigorous. So, while you can never prove the negative—I don't think it's possible to *exclude* occasional visits to the earth by beings from elsewhere—you would have to require much higher authority—data—than any that has been brought forward up to now by the UFO people.

Philip J. Klass, author of the informative book *UFO's Explained,* purports to ascribe natural causes to every sighting and appeared for the negative side of the discussion. However, his book does not solve the dilemma and his views may cause him some embarrassment in the future if the UFO's become properly certified as such.

October 11, 1973

The most startling contact case of recent years happened in Pascagoula, Mississippi, on October 11, 1973. It was given a large segment of time on the TV Special.

Charles Hickson and Calvin Parker, shipyard workers in Pascagoula, reported that a UFO landed near them while they were fishing on the west bank of the Pascagoula River. They were taken aboard the ship by leathery-skinned humanoid creatures and examined by an apparent scanning device which Hickson called "the eye." They were released in about twenty minutes. Parker was little help because he passed out, apparently from shock, according to his report; but Hickson remained conscious and was able to describe his experience in lucid terms.

The full testimony of the men has been repeated many times, and we won't reproduce it all here, but the attitude of the producers of the Special is worth noting. Hickson was interviewed respectfully, and the long list of checks and double-checks on his story was given. The Special stressed that no one, from Dick Cavett on his talkshow, to hypnotists, to police, and doctors, has been able to fault Hickson's report.

That the two men had a harrowing experience of some sort no one doubts. Parker has since resigned from his job and taken up other work in another town, wishing to get completely away from the site of his strange encounter. Hickson, an ex-foreman at the shipyard, seemed a stronger personality and has maintained his residence and his work, but presents an obviously jittery demeanor while recounting the incident.

The two have been examined and re-examined by psychiatrists, government people, and intelligence agents. Their private conversations have been monitored and their backgrounds searched. No one finds reason to suspect them, and it is generally agreed that they would not be capable of perpetrating a hoax of this nature and magnitude. Young Parker would be quite incapable at fooling anybody, and Hickson has been a trusted citizen of his town for many years.

Co-author Zola Levitt had the opportunity of interviewing Rev. William Riddick, a Baptist Pastor from Pascagoula who knows the two men personally. Riddick saw no reason to doubt either of the men, and he personally believes the entire incident. He cites the Biblical concept of demon activity as an explanation.

The Hickson-Parker Case

Several characteristics of the incident suggest unearthly activity, or at least activities completely beyond our grasp. We can understand flying machines and even the "eye" (we use such scanners in airport security searches), but the men report that they were "floated" into the UFO without benefit of stairs, that the creatures who escorted them were not human beings (Hickson's drawings look like monsters from a horror movie), and that the machine exited the scene instantaneously, unlike any conventional aircraft.

Perhaps the most persuasive part of the Hickson-Parker contact case lies in the fact that, as it was stated in a likeable drawl by a concerned citizen of the area, "They're just regular, good ole Mississippi country boys—nothin' more, nothin' less. I couldn't see why they would want'a concoct a story o' that nature, y'know—Hell, I take a drink as much as anybody, and *I* couldn't come up with *that*!"

True enough, Hickson and Parker had little to gain by fraud in a case like this. Parker was badly shaken, and his reclusive activities since the incident rather attest to his very negative feelings about the whole thing. Also, his having passed out and his resultant inability to report very much from the incident is a weakening influence on the story, hardly the work of inventors. It would have been stronger, if the two were perpetrating a hoax, to have Parker come up with a matching story to Hickson's and definitive descriptions. Hickson has gained a bit of notoriety, not all of it positive, but hardly any reward justifying the effort.

Interestingly, however, a sharp-eyed operator of a nearby drawbridge said he saw nothing. He pointed out that he must watch the area carefully for approaching ships, and he had noted nothing at all unusual that night. He did draw the bridge to let one ship through, so it proved that he *was* on the job and watching. He was a bit on the elderly side, but his articulate denials matched Hickson's protestations on the other side. It should also be noted that neither the security cameras nor passing motorists reported anything unusual. This suggests the whole experience was selectively implanted into the minds of the shipyard workers (or a designed hallucination) and not a real event, an idea we will discuss again later. (See Appendix 5)

Pascagoula Sheriff Jack Diamond, accustomed to the personalities of the area, and speaking their language, interrogated Hickson and Parker together and separately immediately after the incident. He feels the story is genuine.

Another persuasive testimony was given on the Special by Astronaut McDivitt, who showed photos he had taken through the window of his Gemini IV spacecraft. Two cameras were floating about the craft, McDivitt said, and he grabbed them when he spotted the UFO outside. He doubts, however, whether the photos he took really show the UFO he saw. They showed a large white oval on the film but McDivitt suspects that was just a reflection from the window. He apparently did not have time to effect the proper camera settings at the moment of the sighting. He does testify absolutely to having seen the UFO, however.

The Special ended with a request by Sen. J. Edward Roush of Indiana that the government create a log of sightings that are reliable, and the announcer stating plainly that "We have a real and persistent phenomenon. . . ."

That last statement, possibly cleared with the Department of Defense, is something new in the way of certification for UFO's, or at least for reports about UFO's. Were a TV Special done on UFO's in the days of Project Grudge, the announcer might have concluded, "And so we see that there's nothing up there after all."

The difference is very significant.

FOOTNOTES

1. Blum, *Beyond Earth,* pp. ii, 224. Several other sources also imply this to be possible or true, eg. Martin M. Singer, Editorial Director, *Saga's UFO Report,* Spring 1974, p. 4; L.J. Lorenzen, director APRO; etc.

1a. Interview with Mr. Galley on a French radio station, reported in *Flying Saucer Review,* vol. 20, no. 2,; pp. 3-4.

2. The National Tattler, Oct. 13, 1974.

3. *APRO Bulletin,* "Something in the Air," July-August 1974.

4. Emenegger, pp. 130-147.

5. *Saga's UFO Report,* Summer 1974, pp. 48-49 for all celebrities mentioned except Goldwater.

6. Emenegger, pp. 100-106, and *Saga's UFO Special,* vol. 3, p. 8, for astronaut sightings.

7. Emenegger, pp. 148-149.

8. *MUFON 1974 UFO Symposium Proceedings,* p. 16 (Quincy, Illinois 62301).

For example, if one wishes to postulate worlds other than the physical (astral or etheric), one can easily satisfy and explain virtually all of the reported antics of the UFO.

J. Allen Hynek,
The UFO Experience, Ch. 12

Is it not at least a little odd that the ufonauts themselves have seemingly gone out of their way to confirm our own guesses as to their origin and purpose?

Jerome Clark
Flying Saucer Review
Vol. 18, No. 5

Everything in their behavior seems designed to make us believe in the outer-space origin of these strange beings and their craft. And, indeed, such incidents have greatly influenced the researchers, who have "independently" concluded that the UFO's are space probes sent by an extraterrestrial civilization.

Dr. Jacques Vallee
Passport to Magonia

Unfortunately, after all these years of research, study, and investigation by thousands of people and scores of scientists operating outside the Air Force and government, there is still no evidence to back up the notion that flying saucers come from outer space.

John A. Keel
Saga's UFO Report
Summer 1974

Up to now (1974), as far as I know we have no indisputable proof of the physical existence of UFO's. There are no easy answers.

Ralph Blum
Beyond Earth

And it is still true that not even one earthlike planet outside our solar system has been observed objectively or is known to exist in fact. Exobiology is still a "science" without *any* data, and therefore no science.

Dr. G. G. Simpson
*Communication with
Extraterrestrial Intelligence*

4

And For Their Next Trick

UFO's embarrass people.

The military and scientific communities are completely confounded the world over, and even the UFO investigatory agencies can't seem to agree on very much. The government is now clearly concerned, but they're as mystified as the rest of us. If the purpose of the UFO's is to drive us crazy with unanswered questions, they're succeeding.

But former CIA director Vice Admiral R. H. Hillenkoetter has said it is "imperative" that we find out the origin and purpose of the UFO's.[1] Few disagree with that.

Gordon Creighton, a distinguished scientific UFO researcher, points out, however, that UFO investigators agree on very little. When it gets down to particulars, there are just about as many theories as there are investigators.[2]

The problem is that UFO information just doesn't add up. The craft refuse to behave in any consistent way. They exasperate the most conscientious researchers, and they persist in baffling the whole world. Dr. J. Allen Hynek says that the characteristics of the UFO phenomena are embarrassing not only when presented to the public and scientific minds but also to the best investigators themselves, if they are honest about it.[3]

The most popular hypothesis by far is the extraterrestrial theory—that the UFO's bring visitors from another planet out there somewhere in space. We are being examined out of scientific curiosity (much as we examine bees or ants), or we are being prepared for an interplanetary "United Nations", or they are getting ready to invade us, etc, etc. We are not entirely adverse to meeting our space neighbors, but we would have expected more comprehensible behavior on the part of an advanced civilization.

Help—If You're Up There

There are many, many problems with the interplanetary-visitor hypothesis. To begin with, we know so very little about the universe that we can't really talk too confidently about what goes on anywhere but here on earth. We don't know how the universe began, scientifically speaking, nor what it's for. We know that it is a hospitable place for men to inhabit, with an incredible number of variables balancing just perfectly for our accommodation, but we don't even know *why* we live here at all. Other than in the Biblical view, we have no satisfactory answers to the origin of the universe or how and why it operates.

The frustration in the scientific community over the "big bang" theory, and other ideas that have come and gone, is so intense that we find, here and there, a sheepish resort to a "creator". *Science News* recently ran an article breathlessly propounding the "certain very special propensities without which we could not exist" in the universe, and concluding that it seemed as if the universe knew we were coming. Though the articles wistfully specified that the creation-by-God theory would solve all the problems, this is not likely to be regarded as a breakthrough.

Given the present unpopularity of God in scientific circles, most scientists approach nature and the universe from an evolutionary angle. Everything was once small and simple and has now become big and complex. The universe was once a single massive particle that exploded and produced large numbers of smaller particles and these in turn have become the stars and planets, etc., that we see around us. Floating gases, dust, and so forth combined and condensed to make the worlds and the galaxies, and on one of these life spontanously appeared.

It's a very good yarn and one that seems to fit the case in some ways, but there's just no way of verifying it. Theories of this sort come and go. Of the eleven main theories of how our own solar system originated, posited since 1644, all have sooner or later been abandoned.[4] The four major theories explaining the origin of the universe have experienced similar fates.[5] The theories only last until something comes along that won't fit; then they are either amended or a new theory is put forth.

Worlds Unknown

Getting down to specifics about the unknown, we have no evidence that there really are any planets out there beyond our own solar system. And if there aren't any planets for the UFO's to come from, then they're not flown by extraterrestrials, assuming extraterrestrials live on planets as earth creatures do. More simply, the normal assumption about the UFO occupants is that they have driven their flying machines from their planetary homes. But the problem is that we have never seen a planet outside our own neighbors in our solar system.

It is a very popular, and maybe even reasonable, notion that there are planets everywhere in the universe. This has always been more or less assumed as an extrapolation from our own solar system. The popular writer Isaac Asimov has described billions of planets circling infinite suns in the universe.[6] NASA scientist Dr. John Billingham believes that there are hundreds of billions of planets in our own galaxy, let alone the rest of the universe, which could have life at least as advanced as our own![7]

But the fact is, we have never seen any of them. We just can't pick them out at such distances. As D. H. Menzel admits concerning the existence of outer space planets, "Any figures you may have heard, including mine, are just guesses."[8]

Spotting a planet even close by, say at a distance of ten light years away, would be the same as spotting a pea at 28,000 miles! And it's not likely that our technology would ever improve sufficiently so that we could see them. Any planets that may be there would be entirely lost in the radiance of their stars.

But assuming, even though we do *not* have the facts, that the planets are really out there after all, we then run into the question of whether they would be able to support life. If the UFO's came from an outer-space planet, there must be quite an advanced civilization out there, capable of intergalactic travel and the impressive array of performances credited to the UFO's.

But for a planet to support even the simplest forms of life is a tall order. The planet must have extraordinarily hospitable accommodations, as the earth does, within precisely defined limits. The earth has exactly the right temperature, the right chemical composition, the right atmosphere, the right gravity, the right position relative to the sun and the other bodies, etc., etc. The tiniest margin of error in virtually any one element of these basic life support systems would make the sustenance of any kind of life at all inconceivable.

But we are now looking not only for a planet where we have seen no planets, but we are looking for life on that planet on a far more advanced plane than what we have yet known. As a professor of chemistry, Donald England warns, "Any speculation as to imaginary men on imaginary planets is pure idle speculation."[9]

Exploding the "Big Bang"

The problem with finding life of any sort out in a "big bang" universe is that we must first bridge the gap between dead matter and primitive life. We haven't space here to go into the enormous case against spontaneous generation—the coming together by chance of precisely the right materials under precisely the right conditions to satisfy the requirements of life. Dr. James F. Coppedge's excellent book, *Evolution Possible or Impossible?* elaborates on the subject. Some scientists have neatly claimed that earth must be the only place where it could have happened. They have thought that once is plenty for so farfetched an occurrence.[10]

The idea of spontaneous generation is based on the lapse of enough time for virtually *anything* to happen. But is this quite fair? One scientist states:

> I should like to discuss . . . what I call the practice of infinite escape clauses. I believe we developed this prac-

tice to avoid facing the conclusion that the probability of a self-reproducing state is zero. . . . These escape clauses postulate an almost infinite amount of time and an almost infinite amount of material (monomers), so that even the most unlikely event could have happened. This is to invoke probability and statistical considerations when such considerations are meaningless. When for practical purposes the condition of infinite time and matter has to be invoked, the concept of probability is annulled."[11]

Or, more entertainingly,

Subject	+	Time	=	Result	Designation
Frog	+	split second	=	Prince	Fairy tale
Frog	+	300 million years	=	Prince	Science[12]

The idea of life emerging spontaneously from non-living materials has always been difficult to reconcile, and it is lately coming under serious fire in the scientific world. It is interesting that years ago the Nobel Prize winner and Harvard Professor Dr. George Wald stated, "The spontaneous generation of a living organism is impossible".[13] Yet he still believes in it because, after all, "here we are". Dr. Duane Gish, who spent eighteen years in biochemical and biomedical research at Cornell University, the University of California, and the Upjohn Company, concluded after his investigation of theories of life origins, "An evolutionary origin of life is impossible".[14]

Taking a cue from the frog and the prince, Dr. Louis Bounoure, Director of Research at the National Center of Scientific Research in France, calls evolution "A fairy tale for grownups".[15] Statements like these could be multiplied a hundred fold. Remember also that the idea of life in outer space is founded upon the theory of evolution.

Mystery Within a Delimma

But getting back to the origins of UFO's and our increasingly improbable search for their outer-space civilization, let us assume that their planet experienced the spontaneous generation of primitive life in the distant past (assuming that their planet was there in the first place). We now have to make another assumption—and a big one. We must assume that they experienced the phenomena of primitive life evolving into more advanced life.

This concept again repeats a series of improbabilities almost as difficult as spontaneous generation. It is perhaps a bit easier to assume that, once life is present, it will advance. But the advancement of simple life into complex life is something fraught with mystery. A sea creature coming up on the land is not so hard to imagine, but how did the human eye evolve? Charles Darwin, in one of his lesser-used quotes, "freely confesses" that the idea of the eye evolving by natural selection is "absurd in the highest degree."[16]

Life is full of such anomalies. The bat has radar so efficient as to make the best efforts of man laughably primitive. Hundreds of other species show characteristics that are theirs alone and without which they could not survive, having apparently not evolved from a lower form.

In conclusion, it is our purpose to study the probabilities of this hypothesis—that the UFO's are the machines of a planetary civilization like our own. That we have to chance over evolution in the process is just a step we must take in our reasoning. We should bear in mind that evolution, like the existence of the outer-space planets, is a hypothesis, not a proven fact. We should also bear in mind that many people believe evolution as fervently as the devout believe *their* religion.

Let's grant, for the sake of argument, that our hypothetical planet, from which the UFO's hypothetically come, did experience the evolution of complex life from the spontaneous generation we granted them earlier. When we accept all those assumptions, we are not nearly finished assuming.

We must now assume that the complex life forms that evolved became humanoid (or man-like in appearance). The Pascagoula observers experienced man-like "monsters" with legs, arms, and faces of a sort. The reported size of most of the UFO's suggest creatures of about our own dimensions, give or take a little. It's a bit sobering to realize, by the way, that if somebody from Jupiter dropped by, and his size were in the same proportion to the area of his planet as ours is to earth, he would rival in size our New York skyscrapers.

Evolution—Not Repeatable

The problem with the step to humanoidism is that the almost infinite variables of the evolutionary path could produce any number of possible creatures. Assuming the evolutionary process, the variety of life on earth certainly testifies to that. We can imagine that if we placed an identical spore of beginning life on numerous planets, with their numerous conditions and life support variables, we would end up after an evolutionary process with a highly varied group. Obviously, the lengthy series of accompanying accidents and mutations could never be expected to duplicate themselves exactly under different circumstances.

The respected scientist George G. Simpson of Harvard has referred to this point:

> Both the course followed by evolution and its processes clearly show that evolution is not repeatable. . . . This essential non-repeatability of evolution on Earth has a decisive bearing on the chances that it has been repeated or closely paralleled on any other planet.
> The assumption, so freely made by astronomers, physicists, and some biochemists, that once life gets started anywhere, humanoids will eventually and inevitably appear, is plainly false. The chance of duplicating man on any other planet is the same as the chance that the planet and its organisms have had a history identical in all essentials with that of the Earth through some billions of years. . . . Let us grant the unsubstantiated claim of millions or billions of possible planetary abodes of life; the chances of such historical duplication are still vanishingly small."
> "The factors that have determined the appearance of man have been so extremely special, so very long continued. so incredibly intricate, that I have been able hardly to hint at them here. Indeed they are far from all being known, and everything we learn seems to make them even more appallingly unique. If human origins were indeed inevitable under the precise conditions of our actual history, that makes the more nearly impossible such an occurrence anywhere else.
> I therefore think it extremely unlikely that anything enough like us for real communication of thought exists anywhere in our accessible universe.[17]

Studies have actually been attempted to try to approach the question of whether we would find humanoid or "monster" creatures on outer-space planets. There does appear to be a relatively uniform chemical composition throughout the universe, but this indicates only that creatures from elswhere would be made up of the same chemicals we are familiar with. Bacteria, lobsters, and apes are made of the same chemicals, after all, but have little in common socially. One study concluded that aliens could not possibly be humanoid, but other scientists have held fast to the humanoid theory.[18]

So, the granting of humanoid form to our assumed neighbors on their assumed planets is yet another rather tenuous assumption. We are beginning to run into that "practice of infinite escape clauses." We just don't seem to have the data to support the popular asssumptions about the UFO's, and while we'd probably like our visitors to bear some resemblance to the human family, it doesn't seem likely.

Don't Bet On It

Dr. Simpson advises that we really don't have much of a case for the UFO's being manned interplanetary visitors of some humanoid type. He wraps up our discussion here incisively:

"Statements in both the scientific and the popular literature that there are millions of such (planetary) systems suitable for life and probably inhabited may give the impression that we know that they do exist. In fact, we know no such thing in any way acceptable as sober science. There are no direct observational data whatever. . . .

[This is] far beyond our present capabilities or any reasonable extrapolation from them. . . . It bears repeating that there are no observational data whatever on the existence, still less on the possible environmental conditions, of planets suitable for life outside our solar system. . . .

There are four successive probabilities to be judged: the probability that suitable planets do exist; the probability that life has arisen on them; the probability that such life has evolved in a predictable way; and the probability that such evolution would lead to humanoids. . . .

And he concludes;

The product of these probabilities, each a fraction, is probably not significantly greater than zero."[10]

All In The Family?

Perhaps our own solar system is the home of the UFO's. Could they conceivably come from a neighboring planet? From the moon, perhaps?

This would solve quite a few problems and give us that "in the family" feeling at least. We might more readily expect that creatures sharing our own sun would have something in common with us. We could more easily conceive how they got here, the distance being so much more reconcilable, and could understand more readily their interest in how we do things here.

But the general consensus is that there is no life in our solar system other than on earth. Clearly, life does not exist on the moon, or at least we haven't seen any. It has been proposed that moon creatures could be living under the surface of the moon or might be invisible, but it's awfully hard to imagine such creatures constructing UFO's and traveling here in them. As we have already said in our demon theory, life may exist on the moon, but our meaning is that demon life may *permeate* our solar system and outer-space, without being "at home" anywhere. Demons are not corporeal and require no physical habitat.

Our recent Mariner 10 probes sent to Venus and Mercury and our Pioneer 10 sent to Jupiter clearly indicate that no life we can conceive of exists in those inhospitable places. After the Viking landing on Mars in 1976, we can add that neighbor to our list of inquiries, but the preliminary evidence for life there looks very doubtful.

Saturn, Uranus, Neptune, and Pluto have been beyond our search to date, but it is hard to imagine life on any of those cold, chemically hostile environments. The big problem, of course, is liquid water. Absolutely essential to life as we know it, water is found only on the earth, as far as we know.

So, as far as has been humanly possible to determine, we are alone in this solar system, and it is likely that we are entirely alone in our universe!

The Unscientific Method

So much for trying to solve the UFO mysteries scientifically. By and large, science doesn't have enough of the answers, and we are reduced to tabulating probabilities of probabilities in our search for answers. Scientifically speaking, we ought not to have any UFO's because there's virtually no place for them to have come from and no reason for them to exist (see appendixes). But we do have them anyway, so we'll have to take the only other reasonable approach, a study of the UFO phenomena themselves. Perhaps in their behavior they reveal some clues about their origin and purpose.

Here again, however, as with our scientific inquiries, we shall find that the information we have doesn't amount to much and reveals no satisfactory conclusion. The behavior of UFO's doesn't suggest anything psychologically relevant to human thinking. They just don't "act" like space travelers or like any human being we know of. In fact, their behavior is benignly inexplicable (at least most of the time)

UFO's seem to play games with humans. They buzz planes and cars and they scare people half to death. Some of the time they seem to conduct relatively intelligent experiments, as with the Pascagoula abduction or the White House observations or the cow of 1897; but most of the time they just seem to sport around in their superior vehicles making mischief. Their unpredictable activities hardly suggest the serious investigation of one planetary society by another. They seem, rather, to be trying to confuse us—and they have.

They never crash. They never make a mistake. They never put down for repairs or refueling. People have reported seeing UFO's crash or stop for what appeared to be repairs, but these sightings are extremely suspect. To date, none of these claims have stood up.

The Rules Don't Count

Our knowledge of machines dictates that if we are going to fly something very high and very fast we're going to have a few headaches. That's just the nature of life on this planet. There are infinite variables that make supersonic travel hazardous or at least make it require occasional maintenance. If "visitors" want to fly around us, we assume they'll have to abide by the natural rules of this planet.

But the UFO's have no problems at all with navigating earth's air space. They go merrily on their way, impervious to capture, detected apparently only when they want to be.

And that's another point. They neither consistently come right out into the open nor do they consistently avoid detection. Some sightings have been blatant self-revelations by the UFO's. Did they think, when they decided to take a break by putting down practically on the shoulder of U.S. Highway 70 near the White Sands Proving Grounds, that we wouldn't notice? Did they suppose that Charles Hickson and Calvin Parker would not mention their eerie experience in Pascagoula? Did they think they could fly in and out of the White House airspace, crisscrossed by excellent radar as it is, without us responding?

When they are pursued by airplanes, which has happened thousands of times, they may hang around a bit before they zoom off. They have closed on many a plane, seemingly for observation purposes, without apparent concern that they had been spotted and were being tracked on radar and duly certified by exceptionally trustworthy witnesses.

And then there's the craft itself—almost with no constant design, according to our observations. Our experience with machines again dictates that it is simpler to design a prototype and then copy it over and over. We have never made a machine capable of both infinite variety and constant performance. Why would we try?

But it's very hard to find any two sightings that agree exactly. Everybody sees something a little different—or a lot different. The idea that some superior civilization builds infinitely varied craft and sends them here only once is unacceptable to any logical mind.

In our wars we are able, through intelligence observations, to understand the various kinds of ships or planes used by the enemy and their capabilities and failings, etc. This is a vital part of combatting the adversary, and we would certainly put it to work in the case of the UFO's. Classification is a routine effort for our military. But we can't proceed in the normal way, because the UFO's just won't fit into any exact or known classification. They seem to have infinite style, body types, capabilities and missions. This *is* frustrating, to say the least.

Now You See It—

We have had some experiences with a peculiar UFO ability to be seen or not seen at will, even by cameras and radar. That is to say, at the same sighting, a UFO can be seen but not photographed, or can be photographed but not seen. One individual sees the craft and tries to take a picture, getting blank film; another just takes a picture of empty sky and comes up with a UFO on the film! With regard to radar, the UFO's are sometimes easily tracked; at other times, though their position is reported, they cannot be tracked!

This phenomenon is too strange even to discuss, but rests on observation, like many of the other characteristics we have been talking about in this section. Capable, experienced observers have noted this inexplicable jamming ability, or super-camouflage device.

Most of the UFO occupants that have been reportedly seen, such as those who appeared to Hickson and Parker, need no space suits or special apparatus for our atmosphere. As proficiently as their machines negotiate our air, the creatures themselves seem to breathe comfortably, according to reports. (We do assume that they breath, since we just don't have any other options.)

Our atmosphere ought to pose other problems to the UFO's, but they seem to have little trouble in that regard. Air friction, at the speeds achieved by the UFO's, ought to be somewhat problematical, especially at supersonic speeds near the ground— another hazardous combination. We must assume the UFO's are made of some heat-resistant material we know nothing about, because this one factor would pose an insurmountable problem for us. Our rockets must carry very specialized heat shields, even for slower speeds at higher altitudes.

Our air is a good conductor of sound, and we ought really to be able to hear some noise when the UFO's go by. In fact, there ought to be sonic booms, but it seems no one has reported any such observation in connection with a UFO. Occasionally we hear of a "whirring sound," but, in general, UFO's are virtually silent, an utterly impossible feature of fast-moving aircraft on this particular planet. If the engines don't make noise, we would at least expect to hear the air resistance. We have heard of crackling and buzzing sounds associated with UFO's, but nothing that could reasonably be interpreted as the sound of propulsion. This is a strange phenomenon indeed.

The reported ability of UFO's to change shape, size, or color, and their propensity for instantly "disappearing" are rather hard to understand also. As we have mentioned, pilots as far back as World War II reported shape-changing fireball craft tailing their planes or flying at their wing-tips.

UFO's that turn up on radar become merely "sources of light" when the jets scramble to pursue them, as over the White House. This metamorphosis, or whatever it is, is quite a disturbing factor.

Another Law

A frustrating propensity of UFO's is that they seem to continually violate inflexible physical laws. That they fly so well at high speeds through thick air without noise is sensational enough, but they break mechanical laws that govern all motion in this particular gravity.

There is a law of mass-ratios that absolutely dictates against the tremendous recurring accelerations routine to UFO flight patterns, if they have an onboard fuel supply. A propulsion machine simply must carry a fuel supply, by all human reckoning, and there is a definite and constant ratio between the original mass of the vehicle and its mass at any subsequent moment due to fuel expenditures. The amount of fuel required for UFO's to do what they do is simply far greater than that which it is possible for them to carry, at their reported sizes.[20]

Furthermore, they do their remarkable accelerations—instant direction-changes and so forth—at speeds which ought to tear them apart, to say nothing of shaking up the passengers. One report clocked a UFO at 16,000 mph, enough to splatter its occupants against the walls with any quick turn and to utterly destroy anything but a fully solid object.[21] We must keep in mind that, while their technology is said to be that of an alien, advanced science, they are doing these tricks right here in our own gravity. Conceivably there exists some other set of physical laws somewhere in the universe, though this is awfully doubtful, but then the craft should fail to work under earth conditions. One would assume, "when on earth, do as earthlings."

It has been said in many connections that the UFO's are actually remote-controlled *unmanned* vehicles. Thus we'd eliminate the problem of the impossible G's exerted on any occupants during an acceleration. But then we should certainly be able to pick up the signals. We have not intercepted anything even remotely like UFO communications or control signals, though we are seemingly capable of that.

Finally, there are the reported instances of fires, teleportations, UFO's "splitting" or "combining", and the like. The unearthly beings—more suggestive of horror-story monsters than extraterrestrials that we would imagine—the occult-seeming "contacts", and the whole supernatural-sounding phenomena reported time and again all suggest something very strange and outside our scientific grasp entirely.

Jerome Clark thinks the "interplanetary visitors" hypothesis is no longer so easy to accept. He says we now know that these phenomena are "infinitely more complex and infinitely less susceptible" to our theories than the believers of the interplanetary hypothesis once so readily accepted.[22] Similarly, Dr. J. Allen Hynek, one of the most respected men in the field, also has problems with the extraterrestrial hypothesis. He says flatly, "There are too many things against it" and refers to the "far, far too many reports" of UFO behavior which pose great problems for the believer in the extraterrestrial hypothesis. Dr. Hynek says that when the solution finally does come, it's "going to be one hell of a quantum jump".[23]

Ufologists have eagerly desired some unifying hypothesis—just an idea of some sort—that would gather in all of the diverse elements of the UFO data once and for all. Scientific inquiry is impotent to explain most of the sightings or the origin and purpose of the UFO's. The characteristics of the visitors themselves leave us baffled.

Thus far in this book, we have tried to explain the problem and to point out that it is real and it is important. We have indicated that we have a unifying hypothesis, albeit an unpopular one. If strong illnesses require strong medicines, then strange illnesses require strange ones. We ask now for open minds to grasp our hypothesis as we approach our solution to the mystery of the UFO's.

FOOTNOTES

1. Blum, p. 87.
2. *Flying Saucer Review,* vol. 16, no. 6, p. 25.
3. Blum, pp. 216-17.
4. George Mulfinger, "Theories of the Origin of the Universe—Examining the Cosmogonies—A Historical Review" in W. Lammerts, ed., *Why Not Creation?* pp. 39-51; J. Whitcomb, *The Origin of the Solar System* (Presbyterian and Reformed, 1964).
5. Ibid., pp. 51-66, in *Why Not Creation?*
6. *Science Digest,* June 1974.
7. *Newsweek,* April 29, 1974.
8. D. H. Menzel, *Aliens In The Skies* (G. P. Putnam's Sons, 1969), p. 194.
9. Donald England, *A Christian View of Origins* (Grand Rapids: Baker, 1972), p. 49.
10. G. Simpson, *This View of Life* (Harcourt Brace and World, 1964), pp. 267-278; H. Blum, *Times Arrow and Evolution* (New York: Harper, 1962), p. 178a; J. Monod, *Chance and Necessity,* pp. 145-146, 180, from F. Schaeffer, *Back to Freedom and Dignity* (Inter-Varisty, 1972), pp. 12-14; Carl Sagan, ed., *Communication With Extraterrestrial Intelligence* (Cambridge: MIT Press, 1973), Appendix B, pp. 362-364.
11. Sidney Fox, ed., *The Origins of Prebiological Systems* (New York: Academic Press, 1965), "The Folly of Probability," by Peter T. Mora, p. 45.
12. Adapted from Duane Gish, *Evolution: The Fossils Say No* (San Diego: 1CR Publishing Co. 1972), p. 5.
13. England, p. 41. From Haynes and Hanawalt (eds.) *The Molecular Basis of Life* (n.d.) p. 339.
14. Duane T. Gish, *Speculations and Experiments Related to Theories on the Origin of Life: A Critique* (San Diego: 1CR Publishing Co., 1972), p. 35 (2716 Madison Ave., San Diego, CA 92116).
15. Dr. E. F. Blick, "Correlation of the Bible and Science," pamphlet. Dr. Blick is a professor at the University of Oklahoma, Norman, Oklahoma.
16. Charles Darwin, *The Origin of Species* (New York: Sutton, 1967), Everyman's Library no. 811, p. 167.
17. G. Simpson, *This View of Life* (Harcourt Brace and World, 1964), pp. 267-268.
18. R. Bieri, *The American Scientist* 52 (1964): 452 "Humanoids on other Planets"; MUFON Symposium 1974, p. 115; Sagan, *Communication with Extraterrestrial Intelligence,* pp. 124, 362-364.
19. G. Simpson, *This View of Life,* pp. 256-259.
20. Aime Michel, *The Truth About Flying Saucers* (New York: Pyramid, 1974), pp. 206-208.
21. *APRO Bulletin,* May-June 1974, p. 9.
22. *Flying Saucer Review,* vol. 16, no. 5, p. 21.
23. Ian Radpath, *Nature,* Oct. 4, 1974, p. 369.

Although, admittedly, there have been more than a few cases in which human beings have been wantonly killed or injured by UFO's. . . .

Jerome Clark
Flying Saucer Review
Vol. 11, No. 5

We are caught up in a series of games which must be played by "their" rules. Anyone who tries to invent his own rules, or breaks the basic patterns, soon loses his mind or even his life.

John A Keel, as quoted in
Creatures From the Inner Sphere
by F.W. Holiday

. . . If your listeners could see for themselves the mess of reports [concerning landed UFO's with occupants] coming in from the airborne gendarmerie [police] from the mobile gendarmerie, and from the gendarmerie charged with the job of conducting investigations . . . then they would see that it is all pretty disturbing. . . . In fact the number of these gendarmerie reports is very great, and they are very varied."

Radio interview with Robert Galley
French Minister of Defense
Flying Saucer Review
Vol. 20, No. 2
Feb. 21, 1974

Many people shy away from everyone who claims to have seen and talked to visitors from other worlds. The natural reaction is to doubt their word, their sanity, or both; yet when scientists and astronomers with the status of men like Dr. W. Buhler, Aime Michel, Jacques Vallee, and Gordon Creighton come forward with a fully documented report of landings and contacts—over 300 of them—between beings from outer space and earth humans, one must reconsider.

From the front jacket of
The Humanoids

Dabbling with UFO's can be as dangerous as dabbling with black magic. The phenomenon preys upon the neurotic, the gullible, and the immature. Paranoid-schizophrenia, demonomania [possession], and even suicide can result—and has resulted in a number of cases. A mild curiosity about UFO's can turn into a destructive obsession. For this reason I strongly recommend that parents forbid their children from becoming involved. Schoolteachers and other adults should not encourage teen-agers to take an interest in the subject. . . . People have actually died after exposure to [the rays] from UFO's.

John A. Keel
UFO's Operation Trojan Horse, Ch. 12

5

The Bible And
The Berkeley Messiah

The Bible is the world's least-read bestseller. It's sort of like one of those books you receive from a book club—you didn't order it, it looks nice on the shelf, and you'll probably keep it, though it's doubtful you'll ever read it. You'll take full credit for having it around the house—it says something about what varied taste you have—but you won't read that one.

Everybody's got fine books they don't read, and the Bible surely heads this non-read bestseller list. But the Bible has an uncanny way of being up-to-date, of being invaluable in understanding the life of each successive generation in this world. Through the years it has been a handbook of literature, history, and poetry, and its moral commentary stands firm after millennia of human stumbling. It has always been able to explain "modern life." Earlier in this generation it explained, for example, the recovery of Israel by God's chosen people and the resulting warfare in the Middle East.

Presently it explains a host of stupefying global phenomena, from inflation and famine to the decline of morality and the institution of ecumenism. Many books on Biblical prophecy have begun to circulate pointing out this mysterious ability of the Bible to illuminate ongoing current events. It is as if someone keeps updating the Scriptures to keep pace with world developments. Our concern here is the UFO's, and the Bible lends knowledge on those, too.

The Bible Tells Us So

We should first understand the Bible as a book of commentary on all phases of life, including the supernatural side. While many people insist that life has no supernatural aspects—what we see is what there is—the supernatural has persistently been with us throughout history. As routinely as forest tribesmen sought medical cures and spiritual knowledge from wizards and magicians, today's police consult psychics to find murder weapons or missing persons. People who claim clairvoyant abilities appear on radio talkshows and "find" lost keys for listeners or tell them their futures. Every city has its diviners who are consulted by the lovelorn and business investors alike. Folks who can detect water or oil under the ground are utilized by drillers with all the sincerity that a cash investment guarantees.

Everybody seems to have those precognitive dreams where one sees a future reality or experiences that weird feeling of "having been here before." Truly there's more to life than meets the eye.

Daniel, Ezekiel, and many other prophets experienced visions which foretold the future with remarkable accuracy. Ezekiel's view of a latter-day alliance between Russia and the Arab nations against a restored Israel is one we can appreciate today (Ezek. 37-39). They commented, as well, about some strange aspects of life for which we have many questions and few answers.

To the Bible writers, the activity of fallen angels, or demons, was simply a fact of life, and they freely gave information about their characteristics and behavior. As we are today witnessing the inexplicable UFO phenomenon, we are going to investigate the relevance of demon activity to what we are seeing.

We have already reported as fully as possible within this space the lack of progress in scientific investigation of the UFO phenomena. In a word, there's little to be gained from this kind of probing. We have turned up almost no cohesive picture of what they are or what they want.

We feel justified, therefore, in making this other kind of inquiry, particularly in this time of revelation about the usefulness of the Bible as a modern-day diagnostic tool.

A Case in Point

We should realize, to begin with, that demons represent an evil force contending against God in the affairs of man. Everybody knows the Garden story, in which the devil took the role of the serpent in order to deceive men and bring sin and death into the world.

The picture is even clearer in the book of Job. God was proud of Job, of whom He said, "There is no one like him on the earth, a blameless and upright man, fearing God and turning away from evil" (Job 1:8). God made this point to Satan, a member of the group called in verse 6 "sons of God" who seemed to doubt that a good man could be found in God's creation. Satan was suspicious of Job, or at least had evil plans for him. He told God that Job's reverence was merely a natural result of his prosperity. "Hast Thou not made an hedge about him" Satan pointed out. "Thou hast blessed the work of his hands, and his possessions have increased in the land" (Job 1:10).

Satan thought that Job's loyalty to God would fall apart if he lost his material possessions. He challenges God, "But put forth Thy hand now and touch all that he has. . . ." Satan feels confident that Job will curse Him to this face.

God gives His permission for the experiment and tells Satan that he may have at Job. He does so, and in the process provides a catalog of demon activities very familiar to UFO watchers. His reported techniques should be of interest to students of the supernatural.

Satan had originally revealed his ability to travel the earth supernaturally when the Lord asked him about his activities—"roaming about on the earth and walking around on it" (Job 1:7). Now he provides misery for Job in ways that ring a bell in these days of UFO activity. In one case a messenger reports, "The fire of God fell from heaven and burned up the sheep and the servants and consumed them; and I alone have escaped to tell you" (Job 1:16). Then in verse 19 Satan's power over the wind runs parallel to several reports of strong winds at UFO take-offs.

Satan has the power to cause Job disease, and the account so states: "Then Satan went out from the presence of the Lord, and smote Job with sore boils from the sole of his foot to the crown of his head" (Job 2:7). (It is interesting to note that mysterious skin infections and painful red welts are not uncommon in certain UFO encounter cases.) But Job remains faithful: "In all this did not Job sin with his lips" (Job 2: 10).

Later, Job's acquaintance Eliphaz tells of his own highly mysterious encounter with supernatural phenomena, a "contact" experience:

> Now a word was brought to me stealthily,
> And my ear received a whisper of it.
> Amid disquieting thoughts from the visions of the night,
> When deep sleep falls on men,
> Dread came upon me and trembling,
> And made all my bones shake.
> Then a spirit passed by my face;
> The hair of my flesh bristled up.
> It stood still, but I could not discern its appearance;
> A Form was before my eyes;
> There was a silence, then I heard a voice:
> Can mankind be just before God?
> Can a man be pure before his Maker (Job 4:12-17).

Eliphaz, coached by this apparition, ends up telling Job to confess his sins, since man is not greater than God. But this is Satan, the subtle one, again. Job's sins are hardly in question and Satan knows that very well. The idea is to further frustrate Job and drive him to remonstrating with God.

Despite the pressure from the supernatural, Job vows in the end, "Yea though He slay me, yet will I trust in him!"

Demon Talent

The doctrinal lesson is clear, but more fascinating for our inquiry is the heavy supernatural evidence in the story. The matter-of-fact presentation of Satan and demon activities in the

Book of Job continues throughout the Bible, showing a compendium of the talents of demons and certainly their evil motivations. From the purposeful deception of Genesis 3, the Garden story, through the Book of Revelation, which deals with our future, demons are prevalent and active.

Millions watched the recent film "The Exorcist," hardly batting an eye at its proposition that a person might, in this age, become inhabited by demons and that this whole thing is essentially a religious, or spiritual, matter. Priests rather than psychiatrists were called on to exorcise the demon, and they invoked spiritual means to effect the exorcism.

We find it believable as theater, but we tend to shrink from it as a UFO explanation. Yet as we examine the Scriptures we find the described activities of the demons to coincide with what we are experiencing with the UFO's in many respects.

Satan is called "the god of this world" in II Corinthians 4:4, and the verse specifies the devil's power to blind men to truth. From the very beginning, Satan has apparently exercised his powers regularly in his war with God. The Egyptian magicians were able to counterfeit the plagues to some degree through their occult practices, according to Exodus 7, and God found it necessary to admonish his own people against the practices of divination and witchcraft (Deut. 18:9-14).

Possession, as a theme, appears countless times in the Bible. The indwelling of human beings by demons is cited in Scripture as producing dumbness, blindness, epilepsy, and a host of other disabilities. (See Matt. 9:32-33; 12:22; 17:15, 18) The demons seek to rest in human bodies (Luke 8:30; 11:24-26; Matt. 12:43-45), including children's bodies (Luke 9:39), and even those of animals (Matt. 8:30-32; Gen. 3:1-5). By way of comparison, possession occurs also in UFO contactee cases, and animals react with sheer terror when UFO's or UFO beings are in the area.

The demons skillfully imitate good spirits (II Cor. 11:14-15) and freely provide occult information, like the prediction of the future (Acts 16:16). They show the ability to manipulate the human mind (John 13:2; Matt. 13:19, 39) and project false realities instantaneously (Matt 4:8). Contactees almost uniformly report (at least initially) the benevolence of their UFO contacts, and they often receive predictions of the future which later, in many cases, prove to be false. They also report the extraterrestrials' ability to exert full control over their minds and perceptions.

Demons have the ability to "prevent" and to some extent control human events and actions (I Chr. 21:1; Dan. 10:13; I Thess. 2:18). They wish to be worshipped (Deut. 32:17; Col. 2:18) and attempt to deceive the whole world (Rev. 12:9; 20:8; Cor 4:4; Eph 6:12). Angels, in general, can assume human form (Gen. 19: 1-11; Luke 1:26; John 20:12; Acts 12:19). They make physical contact with human beings (Gen. 1:10-16; Heb. 13:2) and speak to them (1 Kings 19:5; Acts 23:9; Luke 1:19-20), but they can materialize and dematerialize at will (Luke 2:9, 13, 15). They have tremendous power (Ps. 103:20; 2 Thess. 1:7; 2 Peter 2:11) and can kill men (2 Sam. 24:17; 2 Kings 19:35; I Chr. 21: 12-16; Acts 12:23). Demons, we should remember, are the same as good angels, only fallen. As such, they would have similar powers to the pure angels but would use them for evil instead of good (Dan. 10:12-13). (Demons often appear to occultists in a tangible human form.) All the above-mentioned attributes of angels are also mentioned in UFO reports and contactee cases.[1]

All supernatural beings of the Bible are not evil, of course, and we are warned to "try the spirits" (I John 4:1). Deceptions about God and false gospels are preached by the evil spirits (I Kings 22:19-23; Gal. 1:8; I Tim 4:1; I John 4:1) but good spirits bring prophecy and glad tidings (Dan. 9:21-27).

The Book of Revelation tends to get down to business about Satan's evil plans, since it chronicles the end of the ages. Here we see fire produced from heaven in the presence of men (Rev. 13:13) and terrible torments on the earth (Rev. 9:1-11). The world is deceived (Rev. 12:9) as Satan attempts to bring to fruition his domination of the affairs of men. As in the days of Sodom and Gomorrah, we see tremendous supernatural destruction on earth as powerful angels are released to kill one-third of mankind (Rev. 9:13-21).

It is instructive that all but a few of the seventy-odd powers and abilities attributed to Biblical angels (mostly fallen) are also applicable to the powers and attributes of UFO's or their occupants.

The Berkeley Messiah

Revelation, the final book of the Bible, ties together much foregoing prophecy and gives a cohesive picture of man's future in the world. It's not a very pretty picture, and Biblical analysts feel that this generation should be particularly concerned with it. Our times contain many of the portents of the Biblical "end times", so that the Book of Revelation, formerly thought opaque in its warnings, now gains a real urgency in its appeal.

There's not space here to present the long list of correlations between our times and the prophecies about the end times. Hal Lindsey's *The Late Great Planet Earth,* a book that should be in every home, contains a rather frightening and cogent comparison of the Biblical view and current events.

If the period of Tribulation described in Revelation and other Biblical books is now forming on earth, we should be able to see evidences of the preliminary organization of it. Certain forces should be at work setting up the Antichrist's civilization. It appears that they are and that the UFO's may play a big part in their plans.

Allen-Michael Noonan, leader of a California cult known as The One World Family, is at work producing a twelve-volume *Everlasting Gospel.*[2] He claims to be a Messiah and "the very spirit of the Archangel Michael." He says he is in telepathic communication with UFO's and gets his information from extraterrestrials.

The first volume of the massive work, *To the Youth of the World,* has already been released, along with reviews of the upcoming volumes. In all, the writings seem to be a surrealistic picture of the Book of Revelation, a sort of mumbo-jumbo interpretation of prophecy, but its very relationship to the Bible makes it worthy of a closer look. Noonan seems to be working like crazy to make the most horrible manifestations of Revelation a reality.

Revelations Revealed?

The titles of some upcoming volumes sound like valid prophecy studies—*The Ten Kings, The New World Government,* and *Revelations Revealed.* Ten future industrial complexes will be described in *The Ten Kings,* and *Revelations Revealed* claims to be able to give earth people their future in the manner of the book of Revelation. *The New World Government* is disturbingly suggestive of the era of the Antichrist and rather exactly so, as we shall see.

Of course there are cults and more cults these days, as confused, materialistic people grasp for a spiritual meaning to their existence. But Noonan seems to have a sinister understanding of prophecy and a distinct antagonism toward Biblical Christianity. His doctrine, as we shall see, promotes philosophies very like those we expect to prevail in the coming Tribulation period, and his One World Family is thus worth a second look.

The *Everlasting Gospel* will fulfill the Scriptures, says this messiah, and reveal the true purposes of the UFO's. The "Godhead's" promise of heaven on earth will be realized as the UFO's go into direct action to spread the "Everlasting Gospel" throughout the world. Voting precincts, churches, and temples will be utilized to teach this gospel and to initiate the Worldwide Passive Resistance Movement. Each city will be oriented into the new world structure, says Noonan, and the "agents 666 will do collective buying for each district." Eventually, the "kingdom" will be brought about.

Allen-Michael Noonan claims to have received his "cosmic initiation" in 1947 (that vintage year of UFO sightings, which started the Air Force inquiries), when he was "taken up to the throne of God." He further claims that Venusians from the twelfth dimension summoned him to "help save the world."

Picking through the argot of the cult: "Universal Mind, Galactic Command Space Complex, Jesus factor, placentia planet, artificial tribulation, electric love [telepathy], brain of Minerva [Jupiter], the great quasar, super-God, etc.," one finds a cogent revolutionary system based on both Biblical prophecy and the social perversions of our times.

William Hannaford, the editor of *To the Youth of the World*, claims he was a "contactee" of the UFO's and was "led" to Allen-Michael Noonan. The messiah was experiencing the phenomenon of "automatic writing," where the contacting spirit (or extraterrestrial) moves the pen of the medium. Apparently, however, his manuscript was in need of a rewrite to make it ready for publication! A great many presently popular books, by the way, were produced via automatic writing, according to the authors. *A World Beyond*, by Ruth Montgomery, *Seth Speaks*, and the *Oahspe* volume were all alledgedly dictated by spirits. Similar inspiration was received by Edgar Cayce, Taylor Caldwell, Kahlil Gibran, and Richard Bach, the author of the best-selling *Jonathan Livingston Seagull*. All of these writings and hundreds like them are consistently opposed to the Bible's teaching, as would be expected.[3]

Noonan is aware, of course, of the connection between his doctrine and the Book of Revelation, and he says that his writings have caused him to be called the false prophet, the forerunner of the Antichrist.

He admits that his "Master Plan" certainly smacks of the Biblical view. It does end all buying and selling for secular enterprise, and a new world economy is to be brought about—complete with I.D. cards. But he presents his system as benevolent. For instance, his "agents 666" will demonstrate international healing to a grateful world—everyone who is sick will either be healed or be put on the road to healing in a single day.

As Noonan's Worldwide Passive Resistance Movement grows, his followers will occupy the White House, the Pentagon, the United Nations, etc.; but this will relieve, rather than initiate, a dictatorship, according to the messiah.

The One World Family is off to a rather slow start for its ambitious program. The group presently operates a vegetarian restaurant in Berkeley and is in need of financial assistance.

Would You Believe?

Allen-Michael Noonan's doctrine is a painful amalgam of pop-occult beliefs, socialism, and the happy news that we don't need saving after all. This messiah rather qualifies as a pantheist, seeing God in everybody and everything, but he insists on a wholly new world system. For some reason he refers to Communism as "Christ's communism", and he says the UFO's come from Jupiter and Venus.

In stunning blasphemy characteristic of the coming Anti-Christ, Noonan claims that the being who channeled the writings originally calls himself "I am that I am," the Biblical name of God (Ex. 3:14; John 8:58).

Love, according to his view, is equivalent to Socialism, and universal joy is everyone doing what is natural. Stalin and Hitler are to be forgiven for "eliminating many of the people around them," and the prisons will all be emptied. The United States is the tribe of Joseph, one of the ten lost tribes of the Bible. Every person has his own Godself, human nature itself being divine. God, the universe, "IT" and The Univeral Mind are synonymous terms.

The use of drugs is strongly advocated as a religious rite.

The Holy Spirit of the Bible becomes Noonan's Spirit of Truth, and is available to all freely, being a channel connected with The Universal Mind.

All religions are truth, according to this system, and the inspired (or channeled) writings of Allen-Michael Noonan will provide keys for understanding the scriptures. These scriptures include not just the Bible but all religious, occult, and communistic writings.

The cult believes in reincarnation. There is no sin and no sin nature to be contended with. It follows that there is no judgment. ("The Godhead condemns no one.") People have never needed a savior. The Jesus of the Christian church is not the Jesus the cult claims to know; *their* Jesus is a being of the United Planets Organization of Jupiter. Repentance amounts to dropping out of a mixed-up civilization.

There is much more to Noonan's doctrine, but what has been said is sufficient to describe its anti-Biblical and occult nature. Its UFO and extraterrestrial-related components are rather a sign of the times, but it might just as well give the credit where it's due.

Recalling what we know from the Bible of characteristic demon activity, and supposing for a moment that demons really do exist and are active today, it would seem that they have been passing to Allen-Michael and company exactly what we would expect them to. They provide an antibiblical doctrine and an inspiration to rebel and conquer. They obviously support the Antichrist's kingdom, complete with terminology, and they provide the means (pantheism, occult practices, drugs) for getting there.

The demons demonstrate supernatural powers to inspire their emissaries, whether it be the contact, automatic writings, or UFO's themselves. They confuse the Biblical issues so that the unsaved cannot clearly see the true Gospel: a mind befuddled with drugs or supplied with false definitions of God's own terms is next to impossible to reach for Christ.

Some of what the One World Family believes is harmless nonsense or at least too farfetched to affect the multitudes. That they feel that Sodom was destroyed by a laser beam or that Jesus comes from Jupiter is hardly a cause for alarm among the rest of us. But serious involvement with "extraterrestrials" is something else again, especially since the group insists on promulgating its beliefs among the youth.

Frankly addressing their first volume of "scripture" to "the youth of the world," the cult goes on to advocate the widespread use of drugs, the worship of the occult, and the utter rejection of Christianity. Unfortunately, the uncritical youth of this and former generations have always been fascinated by principles like these without making dogma of them. As things are today, very real dangers accompany the religious claptrap of Allen-Michael Noonan.

We should keep in mind the stated source of the messiah's revelations—the UFO's, via "contact"—as we look deeper into his advocacy of drugs, the occult, and anti-Christism. In the process, we just may be looking at the true nature and purpose of the UFO's.

A Dangerous Trip

To the One World Family, drug usage is a religious sacrament. Drugs are "nature's potions" and "the elixirs of the fountain of youth." The Family intends to set up "proper" usage of drugs throughout the world. Noonan says that taking LSD, psilocybin, and mescalin (hallucinogenic drugs) opens up the "body centers of light."

The danger of drug abuse is minimized, to say the least, and the practice is sold as a healing procedure instead. The drug user is supposedly under controlled "yin and yang" (two cosmological principles regulating the body's positive and negative life forces) and thus cannot harm others or commit serious crimes. Even if the user becomes psychotic, says this pitch, he can only harm himself, and this self-caused pain will teach the user "right procedures." The doctrine explains that "nature's potions" either kill a person or cure him, but that ninety-five percent of the people now using drugs are healed. It is only "the blind who lead the blind" that refer to drugs as dangerous.

Os Guinnes notes a connection between the use of LSD and demon possession,[4] and a statement by the Christian World Liberation Front, in connection with the One World Family, holds that drug use and demon possession may be interrelated. Apparently, contact with "intergalactic beings" in the One World Family is facilitated by the use of drugs. Some of the One World Family have stated that they themselves are not human beings, but extraterrestrials!

This kind of information tempts one to laugh off the whole business as the ravings of a drunkard, or in this case, acid-head. But there is a menacing style and method to this madness, and it correlates very well with what Bible students expect of the end-times world. Drugs unfortunately fit very well into the Tribulation picture, and their advocacy, in spite of all logic, suggests incredibly evil forces at work.

Psychic or Psycho?

The positive attitude toward the occult found in the doctrines of Mr. Noonan also suggests the presence of demons, whose province is the psychic world. The One World disciples claim a history of occult activity, saying that "higher beings," as channels of their Galactic Command Space Complex, would have entered into the bodies of such persons as Hitler, Stalin, and Roosevelt to set the stage for their movement.

The One World "scriptures" include plenty of occult writings and claim a foundation in the Akashic Records, an occult source. They believe that "the occult circles had the greater truths all along." Psychic abilities are considered to be spiritual gifts of great value, and exercises in fortune-telling and automatic writing are respected in the cult. Interestingly, the group has no interest in the subject of demons as recorded in the Bible.

The Spirit of the Antichrist

Christians, regarded as the main threat to uniting the world into one government, will find no place in the coming one-world government. The One World Family is thus in direct opposition to organized Christianity, which they consider the result of "Jesus propaganda." They say that evangelical preaching is of no value at all. The cult refers to the members of the evangelical church as "pseudo Christians" and they advise these to "drop all their thinking about what they think Jesus stood for." The whole Bible, except for some relevant prophecy, could just as well be dropped. The Bible doesn't give any knowledge about what is wrong with people, and if Christians persist in trying to prove their claims, they will seal their doom. The One World Family, on the other hand, pledges to one another that ". . . we are the church of God."

How will the Christians meet their doom? The cult of Allen-Michael Noonan, or its extraterrestrial prompters, puts it this way:

> In order to control the people who persist in doing things that can actually result in disaster for many, though they think they are right, the high beings have developed a righteous secret weapon. . . . [which is] radio-controlled to attack negative vortexes of energies. They are harmless to the righteous people, but those who are out of the discipline and screwing up the works . . . could end up in disaster. . . . All sane people will understand that there must be a way of policing things in the beginning days of our WWPRM [Worldwide Passive Resistance Movement] until we, the World People, have all things under control. . . . No one should have ill feelings about the tactics used by Higher Beings, if necessary, to bring about the right kind of discipline that will bring in our complete New Age.[5]

So we're to have a "passive" revolution, bloody as usual, to usher in a glorious "New Age." The disciples are not to get squeamish about the necessities of dealing with the uninitiated, vision-lacking Christians, for soon everyone will be under "the right kind of discipline."

It would be shocking if it weren't so expected. It's an

intriguing exercise to think of this gibberish in the light of the coming Rapture of the Church. This is the moment described in prophecy when the Church, the members of the body of Christ, are to be "caught up" to be with the Lord (I Thess. 4:16-17). Suppose the foregoing description about the secret weapon is accurate; that would explain the sudden disappearance of the Christians. They were the ones, it will be said, who persisted in the reactionary beliefs that opposed world unification. They all got it from the "Higher Beings." Thus they're gone. "No one should have ill feelings," indeed!

Principalities and Powers

That Noonan and a host of other occult-worshippers have something against Christianity is a kind of evidence that demons are in the picture. After all, Christianity isn't precisely a fearsome force in the world or one that would prevent an upcoming revolution. It has hardly disrupted the dictatorial powers of Russia and China, though it persists in their midst.

But demons have something special against God, as characterized in the Book of Job. Paul indicated that the battles of this world are between "principalities and powers," and we believe that in these times we are uncovering overt demon activity. We think the battle of today is much bigger than, say, some alien planet buzzing our neighborhoods with their flying machines. We think the UFO's represent demon activity come out in the open in these end times.

In the rantings of messiah Allen-Michael Noonan there is a lot of truth. He has hit upon principles of prophecy that are accurate to Scripture, and he has identified Jesus as the true opponent of his heavily occult system. He fits neatly into the Lord's description of false messiahs who mislead many in the latter days (Matt. 24). Like Job, though, the true believers will not falter.

It is important for those who follow God to understand this new and unorthodox attempt of the enemy to gain the world control. This is surely Satan's masterpiece—this confusion of science, Scripture, UFO's, and the occult. This fearsome combination may very well work!

It is important for unbelievers to realize that things are not what they seem. We are not just seeing a phenomenon that science has difficulty explaining for the moment. Strange as it may sound, we are witnessing one of the final battles of the spirits. Soon it's going to be necessary for everyone to choose a side in that battle—or settle for the side that's left.

The idea of active demons being effective in world affairs has long been noted but hardly ever taken seriously. We offer a thought by William James:

> The refusal of modern enlightenment to treat possession as a hypothesis to be spoken of as even possible, in spite of the massive human tradition based on concrete experience in its favor, has always seemed to me a curious example of the power of fashion in things scientific. That the demon theory (not necessarily a devil theory), will have its innings again is to my mind absolutely certain. One has to be "scientific" indeed to be blind and ignorant enough not to suspect any such possibility.[6]

and John Keel:

> Demonology is not just another crackpot-ology. It is the ancient and scholarly study of the monsters and demons who have seemingly co-existed with man throughout history. Thousands of books have been written on the subject, many of them authored by educated clergymen, scientists and scholars, and uncounted numbers of well documented demonic events are readily available to every researcher. The manifestations and occurrences described in this imposing literature are similar, *if not entirely identical,* to the UFO phenomenon itself. Victims of demonomania (possession) suffer the very same medical and emotional symptoms as the UFO contactees. (my emphasis)

FOOTNOTES

1. *Young's Analytical Concordance:* angel, demon, Satan listings compared with a representative sampling of UFO literature and contactee cases (eg., the *FSR, The Humanoids,* etc.)

2. All material on Allen Michael Noonan is from *The Everlasting Gospel,* vol. 1, *To The Youth of The World* (Berkeley: Starmast Publications, 1973), pp. i-16, 59, 73, 97, 107-108, 112, 117, 120-122, 126, 133, 143, 148-149, 130, 194, 211-212, 220, 228, 265-266, 291, 321, 326,

328, 335-340, 345-349, 351 and a statement by Jill Shook, Christian World Liberation Front tract, 1974.

3. Ruth Montgomery, *A World Beyond* (New York: Coward, McCann and Geoghegan Inc., 1971), pp. xiii, 7; Jane Roberts, *Seth Speaks* (Prentice Hall, 1972), J. B. Newbrough, *Oahspe* (London: Kosmon Press, 1942), p. IV-VI; Jeffrey Furst, *Edgar Cayce's Story of Jesus* (Coward McCann, 1970), pp. 9, 10, 19-30; with J. Bjornstad, *Twentieth Century Prophecy* (Dimension, 1971), pp. 69-88, 128-137; with Anne Read, *Edgar Cayce on Jesus and His Church* (Paperback Library, 1971), pp. 107: R. Montgomery, *A World Beyond*, pp. 114-115; Mary Carter, *Edgar Cayce on Prophecy* (Paperback library, 1972), pp. 13-14, 17; Kurt Koch, *Occult Bondage and Deliverance* (Kregel, 1970), p. 24; Gordon Lindsay, *Sorcery in America* (Christ for the Nations, 1968), vol. 2, pp. 19, 26-27; Taylor Caldwell, *Dialogues with the Devil* (Fawcett Crest, 1967), p. 7; Jess Stearn, *Door To The Future* (Macfadden, 1970), p. 176; *Adventures into the Psychic* (Signet, 1971), pp. 178-184; *This Week Magazine,* Oct. 15, 1967; *Ladies Home Journal,* Oct. 1972; Kahil Gibran, *Jesus the Son of Man,* title page; the volume by his secretary, *The Man From Lebanon; Time Magazine,* "It's a Bird! It's A Dream! It's Supergull-! Nov. 13, 1972, pp. 60-66.

4. Os Guinness, *The Dust of Death* (Inter-Varsity, 1974), pp. 298, 300.

5. A. Michel, *To the Youth of The World,* pp. 337-338.

6. Marcie Moore and Mark Douglas, *Reincarnation, Key to Immortality,* (Arcane, 1968), p. 257.

7. John Keel UFO's Operation Trojan Horse (New York: G. P. Putnam's Son's) 1970, p. 215.

[UFO contactee Albert K. Bender's] revelations made no sense to the UFO coterie, since few of them were acquainted with demonology and the fairy myths of the Middle Ages.

John A. Keel
Our Haunted Planet

All these things point to the need for a new tool of investigation to supplement those we already have. This tool is occult science, in the highest meaning of the term. A working knowledge of occult science . . . is indispendsable to UFO investigation. With it, the "contactee" phenomenon assumes a different proportion and an altered meaning.

Trevor James,
Flying Saucer Review vol. 8, no. 1

These [occult] similarities are so remarkable that, after more than two decades of comparatively fruitless research into the UFO enigma, I feel that a new line of approach, from the occult standpoint, might be found to be complementary to existing lines of research and to prove rewarding.

Captain Ivar MacKay
Flying Saucer Review
Vol. 16, No. 4

Without citing scores of cases here, it is possible to realize that the features listed above as pertaining to demons crop up again and again in UFO reports."

Janet Gregory
"Similarities in UFO and Demon Lore,"
Flying Saucer Review
Vol. 17, No. 2

There has recently arisen a growing suspicion that the techniques of the parapsychology phenomena bear strong resemblance to those of the UFO phenomenon itself. It is this suspicion that has motivated a strong body of opinion to campaign for the widening of the terms of reference of UFO investigation to include such subjects as [the] occult, religion, parapsychology, spiritualism, folklore and demonology. What was once thought of as purely an extraterrestrial and physical phenomena has thus become a tangled skein of phenomena whose physical nature and extraterrestrial source are by no means certain.

Jonathon M. Caplan
Flying Saucer Review
Vol. 20, No. 3

The endless messages from the space people would now fill a library, and while the communicators claim to represent some other world, the contents of those messages are identical to the messages long received by mediums and mystics.

John Keel
UFO's Operation Trojan Horse, Ch. 9

6

The Occult Connection

The Berkeley Messiah is an excellent example of the connection between UFO's and the world of the occult. In our search for the plans and purposes of the UFO's, we shall find more than a few instances of this oblique relationship between what appear to be scientific phenomena and definitely unscientific practices.

A number of fascinating, if esoteric, personalities claim an occult connection to the UFO's and the occult in general has seen a tremendous upsurge of interest in our times.

The occult has not only kept up with modern times in this supposedly scientific age but has become a popular facet of modern human behavior. "The Exorcist" was not regarded by the public as a horror story as much as a plausible exposition of reality—a slice of modern life, as it were. Astrological charts and advice appear daily in every newspaper and are consulted casually by the millions. Books on demon possession, contact of the dead or the spirits, and mystical religious experiences, usually Eastern in flavor, are available in every drugstore and supermarket. Occultists, from spiritualists to reader-advisor consultants, maintain offices and cater to the public like pnysicians or dentists.

The Duke Experiments

Parapsychology, often characterized as the serious scientific study of occult phenomena, has gained a certain respectability as a scholarly discipline. Chairs have been established at various universities, and controlled laboratory-style experiments in the realms of the occult go on every day. This work was begun in this country at Duke University by Dr. J. B. Rhine, an established scientist, who published intriguing experimental results from his work with "psi," the psychic ability. Duke set up a true scientific laboratory with facilities for controlled experimentation, where Dr. Rhine pursued the weird world of mediums, telepathists, seers of the future, and those who seem to exercise mind over matter.

The results of the Duke experiments caused controversy among scientists, of course, but were significant enough to attract further experimentation at other facilities, and today many scientists at many labs are trying to track down the elusive phenomenon called "psi." More on that below.

Psychic healing, another occult phenomenon, has been with us from the earliest days of the local witch doctor, but modern times have seen refinements of inexplicable healing techniques taken very seriously, at least by the healed. That psychosomatic illness would respond to the psychoanalyst was accepted grudgingly by the medical world, but the idea of pure faith-healing raised much opposition. Nevertheless, sick people have gone where they could get help, and that has come to include the hypnotist who might solve your ulcer in one session or the psychic "surgeon" who uses incantations and laying on (or "in") of hands.

In the world of astrology, another hoary predilection of human society, computers have been pressed into service, and millions have responded to Sunday supplement ads to have themselves understood by the stars. Like the various techniques of psychic healing, astrological advice and forecasts seem to satisfy the multitudes even though they cannot be found to have a valid scientific basis. Many of our youth would rather know a prospective romantic partner's astrological signs than his family background or tastes. People gladly forward their fees again and again, so that they may plan travel or investments or even marital decisions around the conclusions of the chart-makers.

In books, a good indicator of public tastes, the occult is practically a department of its own nowadays. In the paperback racks, rows and rows of the spirit-contact books or the von Daniken variety sell briskly, and what used to be relegated to science-fiction has almost become social commentary.

UFO's and the Occult

We believe that there is an important correlation between the upsurge of occult phenomena in human society and the increased prevalence of the UFO's. We mean to illuminate this connection, the Biblical ramifications concerning it, and its implications for the future. From a Biblical and historical context, it is clear that the various manifestations of occultism seem to be tied directly to the power of demons.[1] Thus, to the extent that the UFO phenomenon aligns itself with occult phenomena—to that degree it is linked to the power of demons. As believing Christians, obeying Biblical admonitions, we hold to an inflexible position regarding occult phenomena. As thinking members of a global society about to be brought to its fatal denouement by the activity of incredibly evil forces, we mean to sound an alarm.

We will proceed to demonstrate the tie-in between UFO's and the characteristics of the occult phenomena; we will review the careers of certain occult celebrities who, like Allen-Michael Noonan, demonstrate in their activities and literature the connection between the UFO's and the occult. We will show who is behind the UFO phenomena, what they are trying to do, how they are doing it, and why they are doing it. We will discuss the evil involved here and, finally, the Biblical principles that apply to it.

First, the relationship between the UFO's and the occult. We have seen, in considering the powers of the Biblical angels, some evidences of the correlation between occult and UFO phenomena. Some accounts of UFO activities—contacts and various kinds of sightings—seem to run parallel to Biblical accounts, as if the demons of Scripture had stepped right out of the ancient pages and taken up UFO flying.

But this is far from the only connection between the two areas. A great many other occult phenomena have been observed in connection with the UFO's. We are going to consider the physical dangers, deliberate deception by UFO contacts, possession, the interest of the UFO-inspired spokesmen in theology, and various other phenomena associated with both the occult and the UFO's. We will also review the testimonies of contactees, and we will look closely at Uri Geller, the Israeli psychic who claims to get his supernatural abilities from extra-terrestrials. Several studies made by UFO researchers have noted the occult-UFO relationship, and more and more researchers are becoming aware of the psychic correlations that exist.[1] John Keel says that there has always been a "very strong" influence of the occult on ufology. One of the most fascinating books documenting this relationship is Mr. Keel's *UFO's: Operation Trojan Horse*. Originally two thousand pages in length, it is the product of four years of continuous research. It is also noteworthy that many people interested in UFO's in the fifties and sixties ended up involved in spiritualism and various occult societies. Others, recognizing the relationship of UFO reports and psychic phenomena, undertook parapsychological research.[2] Ex-astronaut Edgar Mitchell, as we have mentioned, founded the Institute for Noetic Sciences, which we assume has researched the implications of the correlation between UFO reports and psychic phenomena.

An exhaustive study done by astronomer and computer specialist Dr. Jack Vallee produced a compendium of 923 UFO landings from 1868 to 1968. It revealed that many of them contained the classic characteristics of the more general psychic phenomena, including a strong parallel between "religious apparitions, the fairy faith, reports of dwarf-like beings with supernatural powers," etc.[3] These entities were linked to occult ritual.

A three-year UFO investigation by Brad Steiger, author of over thirty books on occult subjects, contains correlations between UFO and occult-psychic phenomena in at least thirteen different areas, including telepathy, clairvoyance, and heightened psychic abilities on the part of contactees.[4]

In 1969 the United States Government Printing Office issued a publication researched by the Library of Congress for the Air Force Office of Scientific Research: *UFO's and Related Subjects: An Annotated Bibliography.* The senior bibliographer, Lynn E. Catoe, had read thousands of UFO articles, books and publications in preparing the 400-page volume. On Page IV of her preface to the book she has a very significant statement:

"A large part of the available UFO literature is closely linked with mysticism and the metaphysical. It deals with subjects like mental telepathy, automatic writing, and invisible entities, as well as phenomena like poltergeist [ghost]manifestations and 'possession'. . . .

"Many of the UFO reports now being published in the popular press recount alleged incidents that are strikingly similar to demoniac possession and psychic phenomena which has long been known to theologians and parapsychologists."

Finally, in reviewing dozens of UFO books and scores of articles in the *Flying Saucer Review,* considered the finest UFO magazine in the world, I found nearly 300 incidents which showed an interrelationship among UFO phenomena and occult phenomena in general. For a partial listing see Appendix 5

Getting in Touch

Contact with the UFO's often seems to be by occult means. Our visitors have rarely responded to any standard approach, whether it is by aerial pursuit or a ground confrontation. *By contrast, the standard tools of the occult have reportedly established contact in innumerable cases.*

The ouija board, tool of an innocent-seeming, fortune-telling parlor game, is widely utilized by psychics and occult practitioners as well as by the general public. Occultist William Blatty, author of *The Exorcist,* has a healthy fear of it, however, for he refers to the ouija board as very dangerous and says that mental institutions "are loaded with people" who got involved with the occult through using it.[5] In one case of contact with extraterrestrials, two men claimed to be in touch with beings from Mars by using a shortwave radio and a ouija board. Eventually the messages came through by automatic writing.[6]

Some of the old-fashioned mediums are able to act as competent UFO contactees, much as they claim contact with the departed for paying customers. The Solar Light Center claims to be in touch with beings from several planets in our own solar system. The director, Marianne Francis, receives her communications from the extraterrestrials in a manner described as similar to the "way a medium serves as the channel for spirit communication" during a seance.[7]

Brad Steiger mentions another group called The Light Affiliates, who were reportedly contacted by an extraterrestrial named OX-HO. The young girl whom OX-HO used for his contact acted in a way similar to a medium during the communication periods. Significantly, Steiger wonders whether the extraterrestrials would not be termed "spirit guides" by more conventional mediums. He also notes the close similarities between contactee behavior and the behavior of a medium while in a trance.[8]

The idea of dreams being the means of spirit contact is also common to both UFO reports and occult practices. Information and guidance apparently may come to the medium or the contactee during sleep. "Seth," the spirit who has the title role in Medium Jane Roberts' books, has claimed that he and other spirit beings have communicated through Roberts by means of her dream states. He told the medium that she was trained by them for her trade in that manner.[9] As with Allen Michael's The Everlasting Gospel, ideas and even whole volumes can be implanted by spirit beings into the minds of those involved in the occult. The *Urantia Book, A Dweller Between Two Planets,* and *History of the Origin of All Things* are occult volumes allegedly "written through" human mediums by spirit beings or in the first case extraterrestrials.[10] The usual method is automatic writing, although variations are sometimes employed (trance dictation with Edgar Cayce, automatic typing with Ruth Montgomery). The "automatic" part indicates the guidance of the occultist by the spirit, whatever the particular technique. The receiver's thoughts and actions become manipulated from without.

Jonathan Livingston Seagull was written by Richard Bach in a somewhat similar manner, according to his own testimony, and is rather a case of literature than a frank occult discussion, showing the subtlety of the spirits.[11]

Abducted policeman Herbert Schirmer testified that UFO occupants planted "data" in his mind and told him that they do the same with everyone they contact.[12] There is some historical record of occultists receiving very advanced technical information via contact with spirits.[13] Jacques Bergier records a large number of cases involving supernatural beings, or "creatures of light", whose sole desire was to impart advanced knowledge of philosophy and various academic data. They appeared in large numbers during the five centuries between 1000 and 1500 A.D. In the thirteenth and fourteenth centuries they appeared in connection with the Freemasons, a group which later held a belief in extraterrestrial life.[14]

UFO occupants have sometimes become visible entities, as in the Pascagoula abduction, and have made contact directly by "voice," light beams, and "tele-thought".[15] While these testimonies come under much suspicion, they have been plentiful and bear many subtle characteristics in common.

The Professor Speaks

Dr. R. Leo Sprinkle, Associate Professor of Psychology at the University of Wyoming, and a top scientist on the *National Enquirer's* Blue Ribbon Panel on UFO's, recently completed a five year investigation of eighty-two people who reported contacts. Sprinkle found that these involved a normal selection of people of diverse middle-class backgrounds who were psychologically stable. Communication was achieved with the UFO occupants by various means—telepathy, visions, dream contact, "mental voices". Under hypnosis the subjects were often able to reveal very exact details of their experiences, while one man seemed to be under some form of post-hypnotic suggestion by the extraterrestrials.

By and large the subjects got their information from mentally perceived voices, a common occult phenomenon. Dr. Sprinkle remains convinced that some sort of communication is definitely occurring, and he urges that more in-depth studies of the whole situation are warranted by his preliminary findings.[16]

Occasionally information received by mediums from their "spirit controls" concerns the UFO's themselves. Often the data confirms the reality, place of origin, or some other aspect of a UFO encounter. It might take the character of a public relations program for the UFO's, stressing that they are here to save us from self-destruction. Eric Norman lists nineteen mediums and psychics who claim to be receiving messages similar in content to those which UFO contactees receive.[17]

The extraterrestrials are "anxious to teach us," assert the psychics, provided, of course we develop our psychic abilities to communicate with them. Katherine Sabin said some have taken human form and walk among us, while others may have taken control of "several key world figures." Jacqueline Eastlund said the visitors would "take over," if necessary, by controlling people in power.[18] One is reminded of Noonan's Passive Revolution in these threats of enforced benevolence: but it is remarkable how well people will follow a mystical, especially extraterrestrial, ideal. A whole church was founded upon the experiences of Swedish mystic Emmanuel Swedenborg, who claimed to have regular visits from "angels," to have visited heaven by astral projection, and to have spoken to spirit beings from the planet Mercury.[19] His Church of the New Jerusalem is consistently anti-Biblical, it hardly bears mentioning.

Beware the Black Magic

As we look more deeply into occult practices and try to correlate them with reported UFO experiences, we risk an increasingly skeptical attitude on the part of today's society. The public at large does not realize how prevalent occult activity is today nor how debilitating it is to a society founded upon generally Biblical principles. If we bring up the rituals of "black magic," for instance, we will be thought lunatics for giving this area serious consideration.

But frankly, black magic and many other ritual occult practices are going on in every sector of this nation and the world, and they seem to provide illumination for the UFO question.

Most people will concede that if occult practices really work, they are evil. If blood-drinking black masses really do raise spirits, nothing good is behind them. If people are contacting spirits, or at least carrying out instructions of spirits they fancy that they contact, they are not going to make the world a better place.

Well, the occult activities really *are* going on, they really *do* produce some strange effects, and those effects are very reminiscent of the effects produced by the presence of UFO's. Something is up, and it amounts to more than the hair on your neck. Considering the field of serious magic, ufologist John A. Keel has drawn a close parallel between the sinister acts of the Illuminati Cult (related to witchcraft and black magic) and certain UFO phenomena.[19a] In his research on the occult and magic practices of John Whiteside Parsons, a rocket fuel scientist deeply involved in ritual, he notes the presence of power failures, strange glowing lights, and temporary paralysis, all common in UFO reports. Parsons was given several prophecies by his contacts, but he died in an accident, one of the high number of fatalities among those dabbling in UFO contacts.[20]

Magic ritual utilized to conjure up an angel or spirit is commonly attended by nausea and actinic burns, with proximity to the spirit, identical hazards "to those reported by low-level UFO witnesses."[21]

The Qabala, a secret tradition of mysticism, offered certain privileged initiates the capability of communing with "aerial people." Qabalism is considered one of the three Master Rituals in magic practice, and reportedly producing effects quite parallel to those associated with UFO's. Swirling clouds of vapor and rays of light are seen, and the practioner may experience possession or psychic assault.[22]

Some magic rituals conjure "elementals," which are thought to be psychic creations of the magician's mind and which can be sent to torment or murder people. Elementals are so called because they can take any size or shape imaginable, from a man to a giant sea anemone. It is tempting to draw an analogy between the UFO's (or their occupants) on one hand and the elementals on the other. This would explain the infinite variety as well as the sinister purposes involved. Or more simply, suppose the elementals of magicians and the UFO's were the same thing—standard Biblical demons as of yore. That would explain everything.

Possession and the "Kindly Persuaders"

Possession is a major theme of magic and other occult practices and, of course, is also found among the UFO contactee reports. Our contactee neighbors don't merely report communication; they normally have messages of some weight about religion, world takeovers, and the like. They broadcast the kindly persuasions of the UFO folks and their plans to bring us peace on earth. They are not merely "in communication"; they are sometimes truly possessed, and in the worst sense of the word. They are mouthpieces rather than reporters.

There are probably several thousand documented cases of possession in the annals of psychic and occult research, many reminiscent of UFO contactee phenomena. Several ufologists refer to possession in their investigations, and John Keel likens the typical hazards of occult practices—physical attacks by invisible hands, possession, insanity, and hallucinations—to the problems encountered by some UFO witnesses and contactees. The two phenomena, he says, are "inexorably linked,"[23] Another investigator, author Eric Norman, has personally examined eleven cases in which people were "seemingly possessed by UFO entities."[24] Steiger refers to a group of extraterrestrials who claim to be able to possess human beings and to help them with astral projection, or out-of-the-body travels.[25]

Jane Roberts alleges that Seth, her spirit contact, inhabits her and takes control of her body. Seth has dictated six thousand pages of material through his hostess (some of it similar to that reported by certain UFO contactees), and has helped her with astral projection.[26]

Keel also asserts that the dangerous kind of possession usually associated with witchcraft and black magic "is apparent in many UFO contactee cases." He refers to "a number of senseless murders" which were reportedly ordered "by Martians or space people."[27]

"Teleportation," whereby an individual is mysteriously transported from one location to another, and "telekinesis," the transporting of material objects, are also common to both occult and UFO literature.[28]

Interestingly, UFO contactees often have a history of psychic abilities or an interest in the occult. Joan Howard, a medium for most of her life, reports a "training period" she underwent. Space entities "Zio" and "Motag" visited her by night and taught her for a period of some eight months. The visits were astral (non-physical), according to the medium, and had to do with training her to more easily achieve contact and psychic control.[29] Before entering the UFO field, contactee George Adamski headed up a mystical cult, the Royal Order of Tibet.

The Proceedings of the 5th APRO UFO Symposium of June 15, 1974, gives another case of a contact experience with an individual who had experienced lifelong psychic phenomena. The individual continued to experience "hauntings" following the contact with landed UFO occupants.[30]

Because Their Deeds Are Evil

Darkness is common to both UFO's and the occult. Coven rituals among witches, black magic ceremonies, seances, etc., are invariably performed at night or in darkened rooms. Much of the automatic writing experienced by occult adepts occurs between 2:00 A.M. and 4:00 A.M. Similarly, UFO's prefer the night hours. Information from the Aerial Phenomena Research Organization, John Keel, and several others establishes that the vast majority of sightings are at night.[31]

The ability of alien spirits to control events in human lives, as experienced by Job, is also common to both the occult areas and UFO contacts. UFO entities seem to work selectively and deliberately in the lives of certain people, if we are to believe the reports.[32] Allen-Michael Noonan might be an example of one "chosen" to a task. Similary, the occult spirits seem to choose a person as a vehicle and proceed to control that person to certain ends.

In summary, reports of occult practices and reports of UFO-related phenomena have a lot in common. We must understand, of course, that in both areas we are relegated to relying on "reports", or at least investigations by interested parties. There is no scientific laboratory, in the sense of a chemistry or biology laboratory, which reproduces the phenomena of either area, and we cannot verify what we are calling supernatural events on charts or graphs, though parapsychology laboratories do utilize polygraph machines (lie detectors) to verify results of experiments.

On the other hand, what is not "natural" cannot be expected to yield to the methods of natural science. Where science is concerned, UFO phenomena and occult phenomena simply cannot exist. Yet they do exist, as we have seen, and are corroborated by hosts of reliable reporters.

That the UFO's are up there and that they do what they are reported to do is *scientifically* impossible, we might as well say, since the UFO's violate every sort of scientific principle. But they are there all the same, according to photographic and motion picture evidence, radar, human observation, and finally the government, via the TV Special reportedly done with its blessing.

The occult connection is the first hint of a system or a logic to the UFO's and their activities. That they behave in some way related to something we have already noted, however strange and repulsive that something is, is comforting in a sense. By looking carefully at the occult practices, we can at least begin to describe the UFO phenomena in terms of something familiar.

The MacKay Papers

Captain Ivar MacKay, Chairman of BUFORA, the British UFO Research Association, is the author of two carefully researched articles entitled *UFO's and the Occult.* [33] A serious student of occult and spiritualistic physical phenomena, Captain MacKay has noted the many areas of correlation between the occult and the UFO phenomena. His conclusions help tie together what we have already noted in the way of an occult connection.

It should be made clear that Captain Mackay is a conservative among UFO investigators and takes a highly skeptical view of many of the contactee cases. Despite his negative opinion of what he calls "the lunatic fringe UFO cults," he still finds a high level of correlation between occult phenomena and some of the more generally accepted UFO sightings and reports within the investigative community. In that he discounts the prolonged mediumistic kind of contact cases we have been outlining, it is very interesting that he still finds a correlation valid. Captain MacKay believes that studying UFO data in light of the occult could be rewarding, but he sounds a warning as well. He is aware of the "disastrous harm" that seems to follow those looking into the occult, which is "only too apparent among some researchers in recent years."

Unfortunately we cannot reproduce here the Captain's many striking examples of UFO occult similarities, but we will mention the highlights of his discoveries. There are literally scores of subtle ways in which the two areas correlate. What follows is a summary.

Extremely foul odors, like sulphur and ozone, are associated with both seance rooms and "badly haunted" locations. They are common as well to UFO landing sites. Contactees also note the odors in connection with extraterrestrial encounters.

The aversion to strong light in both areas is notable. The UFO's actually seem to take evasive action when confronted by strongly focused light. Supernatural manifestations relative to seances and other occult exercises invariably occur in the dark or in dimly lit rooms.

A sudden decrease of temperature is associated with UFO contacts and in many types of occult occurrences as well. Either the body temperature drops or the temperature of the local environment. People who have penetrated ghostly beings have noticed a distinct chill.

The creatures seen by both UFO sighters and seance attendees are shadowy, transparent, or semi-solid figures, rather more like apparitions than real creatures.

Mentally detected voices are heard in both UFO and occult contexts, the contactees claiming that these represent communication with extraterrestrials and the occultists with various spirits. (The latter claim contact with the dead, which, as with all occultism, involves contact with demons, who impersonate the dead in order to give a false view of the Bible and the afterlife. A particularly enlightening study on this in Raphel Gassons' *The Challenging Counterfeit*.)

The transporting of human and non-human objects by inexplicable means is common to both fields, as is levitation, or the lifting up of a person or thing without physical means. UFO's have reportedly lifted and dropped cows, cars, and other objects, and on-the-spot observers have experienced a feeling of being "drawn" toward or up to the craft. The Pascagoula abductees reported entering the craft through a door high above the ground without stairs or ramp, or, as they put it, "floating" into the craft. UFO observers have reported seeing occupants levitate into their craft. Levitation is a mainstay of seance events, of course.

Sudden appearances and disappearances are common to both fields also, with UFO's vanishing while in plain sight or instantly materializing in an empty sky.

Bursting balls of light and buzzing, whirring, whining, humming, ringing, or chiming noises reportedly accompany both phenomena and signal the approach of a spirit on the occult scene.

The disconcerting lapse in behavior of common physical laws is also a feature of the areas under consideration. We have discussed the rather phenomenal abilities of the UFO craft. In seances the apparitions are similarly impervious to weapons of any sort, can travel through solid walls, or are able to absorb matter into other matter.

The weird UFO photography effect, where objects unseen appear on film or photographed objects fail to appear, is also true of photography in the occult world. The visible subjects in both fields, whether they be UFO craft or the ectoplasmic manifestations in seances, also demonstrate an inexplicable ability to enlarge or reduce in size. UFO's have grown from pinpoints of light into large semi-solid objects and then back down to pinpoints and oblivion.

The effects felt by human beings exposed to encounters in both areas are similar, as we have discussed. The sense of coldness, tingling or prickly sensations, partial or full paralysis, a feeling of buoyancy, the sense of being controlled, and fear are common to both experiences.

Poltergeists, those "playful" spirits whose good-humored haunting of houses has confounded investigators for many years, have been connected with the UFO flaps. John Keel plotted a graph of poltergeist reports and UFO flaps made for the years 1900-1913 and found them highly coordinated. Poltergeist flaps seem to precede, closely follow, or occur simultaneously with UFO flaps.[34] Bishop Pike experienced the poltergeist phenomena—lights going on and off, doors slamming, footsteps, etc.—after his son committed suicide. He eventually consulted a medium through whom he claimed to talk with his dead son. The 5th APRO UFO Symposium mentions one case of a "horrible" UFO experience in which the person involved had her apartment haunted for a long period after the incident.[35]

Where poltergeist effects are concerned, not to mention the myriad other occult phenomena, investigators have felt convinced that demons are responsible. Dr. Merrill F. Unger's study *The Haunting of Bishop Pike,* John L. Nevius' classic, *Demon Possession,* and the writings of the noted authority Dr. Kurt Koch all take this position.[36]

Earthquakes and tremors bear a relationship to both UFO's and the occult. UFO sightings correlate with earthquakes, often occurring just before or during a tremor. In occultism it is believed that fissures in the earth's crust can set up weak spots in its psychic envelope, which allow other intelligences to come through. The weak spots are termed "gateways" by the occult practitioners.[37]

Many more examples would continue to demonstrate a high degree of correlation between UFO reports and occult phenomena. The available data is too lengthy to appear in full here, but the conclusions are obvious.

The volume of literature collected in both UFO and occult areas is immense, so that even a short study of the literature reveals a close coordination between the two.

We hold that the literature studied by Captain Mackay and many others describes valid phenomena present on the earth and affecting the lives of millions; and we hold that the correlation between the two strange areas is explained by the Biblical theory of demon activity. The powers of the fallen angels, which we have described, the presentation of demon activity in Scripture, the impending Tribulation period characterized in prophecy—all suggest the Christian world outlook.

From the Biblical point of view, nothing that is happening is strange or even unexpected, as we will demonstrate. All of what we are witnessing in the fields of the occult, the UFO's, the false messiahs—even inflation and famine—lines up well with what the prophets expected of the period known as the end time. True Christians, with their faith in things unseen, are never staggered by the idea of invisible forces of evil, and they are the last either to doubt or fear the strange phenomena of this age.

FOOTNOTES

1. Merrill Unger, *Biblical Demonology* (Scripture Press, 1971) and *Demons in the World Today* (Tyndale, 1972); T.K. Desterreich, *Possession: Demoniacal and Other* (New Jersey: Citadel Press, 1974)).

1a. McWane, p. 170 (who calls the correlation "frustrating"); Blum p. 225, who notes it would explain "countless" sightings; Caplan observes the "strong resemblance" (FSR, vol. 20, no.3, p. 22); Creighton, who says all occult records should be re-considered in light of UFO phenomena (FSR, vol. 11, no. 4, p. 24); Dr. Edwards, who notices the correlations to ghost and ESP phenomena (FSR, vol. 16, no. 5, pp. 18-20); Charles Bowen (FSR, vol. 16, no. 5, pp. 23-24); Janet Gregory (FSR, vol. 17, no. 2, pp. 32-33) and others.

2. Keel, *Our Haunted Planet*, p. 128

3. Jacques Vallee, *Passport To Magonia*, pp. 66, 110-111, 116-129, 102, 148-149, 56-57, 40, 152-154, 158-163; and cases 2,3,48,51,57,67, 68,70,71,72,82,85,88,94,95,97,101,etc.

4. Brad Steiger, *The Aquarian Revelations* (New York: Dell, 1971), pp. 11-16 and throughout the book.

5. *San Francisco Chronicle*, Jan. 5, 1973, and *The National Observer*, June 1, 1974, for a case of ouija board-related vampirism.

6. Wilkins, *Flying Saucers Uncensored*, p. 40; Jay David, ed., *The Flying Saucer Reader* (New York:Signet, 1967), pp. 81-89; Keel, p. 121.

7. McWane, pp. 121-122; Wilkins, pp. 46, 133-134.

8. Steiger, pp. 18, 19, 58.

9. Jane Roberts, *Seth Speaks* (Prentice Hall, 1972), pp. 38, 351.

10. *The Urantia Book*, (Chicago Urantia Foundation, 1955), pp. 1209-1219; L.M. Arnold, *History of the Origin of All Things* (Kentfield: W.M. Publishing Trust, 1961), p. 418, respectively.

11. *Time*, Nov. 13, 1972, pp. 60-66.

12. Blum, p. 113.

13. Howard Menger, *From Outer Space* (New York: Pyramid, 1974), p. 166; *Saga's UFO Reports: Flying Saucer Review* issues; any number of occult societies and parapsychological associations; R. Brown's Unfinished Symphonies; the Patience Worth revelations, etc.

14. Bergier, pp. 90-98.

15. Steiger, *The Aquarian Revelations,* pp. 93-95.

16. *National Enquirer,* Sept. 27, Oct. 2, 1974.

17. Eric Norman, *Gods and Devils from Outer Space* (New York: Lancer, 1973), pp. 62-82; Wilkins, pp. 46, 133-134; Drake, p. 15; "The Galaxians" tape from The Academy of Atlantis, a Los Angeles occult Society.

18. *National Enquirer* interview with six psychics on the topic of UFO's, March 3, 1974.

19. Raymond W. Drake, *Gods and Spacemen in the Ancient West* (New York: Signet, 1974), p. 10; Walter Martin, *Kingdom of the Cults* (Minneapolis: Bethany, 1970), pp. 242-246.

19a. Keel, pp. 166-172.

20. Ibid., pp. 127-128.

21. Ibid., p. 162.

22. Blum, p. 43; P. Conway, *Magic: An Occult Primer* (New York: Bantam), ch. 7: The Master Rituals; *FSR,* vol. 16, no. 5, pp. 24-25. ("transcendental qabalism")

23. Keel, p. 162.

24. Norman, p. 120.

25. Steiger, p. 85-86.

26. Jane Roberts, *The Seth Material,* pp. 72, 182, 188-189, 228; *Seth Speaks,* p. 184.

27. Keel, p. 128.

28. *Flying Saucer Review* Volumes; Wilkins, pp. 98-101, 223; parapsychological research annals, etc.

29. McWane, pp. 123-124; George King, ch. 7; Puharich, *Uri,* pp. 155, 159.

30. *APRO Symposium,* June 15, 1974, pp. 16-17.

31. McWane, p. 73; *APRO Introductory Bulletin,* "Invitation-Facts,"

32. Steiger, pp. 31, 39, 65, 92; *FSR* vol. 11, no. 5, p. 28; *Saga's UFO Report,* Spring 1974, p. 62; Keel, p. 162.

33. Ivan Mackay, *Flying Saucer Review,* "UFO's and the Occult," vol. 16, no. 4, pp. 27-29; no. 5, pp. 24-25.

34. *FSR Special Issue* no.2, p. 17; Keel, p. 126; McWane, pp. 134-142; *FSR,* vol. 16, no. 5. p. 29.

35. APRO Symposium, no. 5, p. 18.

36. Kurt Koch, *Between Christ and Satan* (Kregel, 1962); *Occult Bondage and Deliverance* (Kregel, 1968); *The Devils Alphabet* (Kregel, 1969); *Christian Counseling and Occultism* (Kregel, 1972); M.F. Unger, *Demons In The World Today.*

37. See also *FSR,* vol 20, no. 1; C. Poher, "Time Correlations Between Geomagnetic Disturbances and Eyewitness Accounts of UFO's," pp. 12-17.

Actually, the history of mediumship is littered with accounts of such (UFO) contact; . . .

D. Scott Rogo in
The Amazing Uri Geller

For some years past it has been increasingly obvious that the very kernel of our problem is the so-called 'contact-report,' so incredible, so baffling, that the instinctive reaction of sane folk has been to fight shy of it altogether.

But we cannot ignore it, because it is virtually all the material we have to work with, It is the 'contact story' and not the 'Flying Saucer story' or 'UFO report' that we must endeavor first to understand. If and when we have grasped what these tales of 'landings' and of 'contacts' with entities mean, we may (perhaps) be on the road to understanding some of the larger aspects of the problem.

Gordon Creighton
The Humanoids

To me it is odd that the people who study psychic phenomena-the parapsychologists-have seldom gotten into ufology or given it any credence.

Dr. B.E. Schwartz
5th APRO Symposium

The central question in the analysis of the UFO phenomenon has always been that of the controlling intelligence behind the objects' apparently purposeful behavior.

Jacques Vallee
Passport to Magonia

Dr. Pucharich: "Are you of the Nine Principles that once spoke through Dr. Vinod?"
"Yes. ["God is nobody else than we together, The Nine Principles of God."]
Dr. Pucharich: "Are you behind the UFO sightings that started in the United States when Kenneth Arnold saw nine flying saucers on June 24, 1947?"
"Yes."

Uri Geller's space contacts answering
the questions of Dr. Puharich in *Uri*

Over and over again, witnesses have told me in hushed tones, "You know, I don't think that thing I saw was mechanical at all. I got the distinct impression that it was *alive.*"

John Keel
UFO's Operation Trojan Horse, Ch. 7

Testing The Spirits

Jesus foresaw ·false prophets in the end times who would lead many astray, and to the wise he gave a word about testing these spirits. In the world today there are a number of powerful or fascinating quasi-religious leaders, usually occult practitioners, who are able to gather followers and promote a doctrine. We have already looked at the strange cult of Allen-Michael Noonan, a typical example. The "best" are yet to come, however.

The Only One to Save Mankind

No one quite knows what to make of Uri Geller. This fellow is either a master magician, a psychic of extraordinary powers, a "21st century man", or a fake. He has been given all of these appelations and more.

Geller's specialties mainly involve incredible feats of mind over matter. It is alleged that he has mentally stopped department store escalators and mountain cable cars,[1] moved the hands of a watch without touching it, repaired malfunctioning electronic circuitry by mind power, formed an image on film sealed in a light-tight camera, bent metal bars without contact or by stroking them lightly (one was ¾" steel, requiring 25 tons of force), "erased" patterns from video tape, made objects disappear and then reappear at another location, and demonstrated an inexplicable psychic control over mechanical devices ranging from laboratory instruments to radios, TV's, audiotape recorders, and even computers.[2] His amazing demonstrations have been studied by the Stanford Research Institute, UCLA, and any number of scientific and lay investigators.

Geller claims to derive his powers from extraterrestrials. In a television interview with Kelly Lang on "The Tomorrow Show," June 18, 1974, he stated that the source of his power came from outside himself and that he was a "channel." In an article in *Psychology Today* he was quoted as saying that the energy coming through him was intelligently directed from another universe.[3]

One of Geller's most fascinating exercises came aboard a flight on a commercial 747. He reported that his Nikon F camera, which he had stowed on the floor beneath his seat, levitated or "floated" up to waist level. He took this as a sign that he was to take pictures of something. He aimed the camera at the empty sky outside his window and took several pictures. Other passengers and the flight crew certified that the sky was completely empty. When the film was developed, five frames contained what seem to be images of UFO's.[4]

Geller has attracted a great deal of attention by his demonstrations. While Allen-Michael Noonan mainly just spouts philosophical jargon claiming extraterrestrial inspiration, Geller actually *demonstrates* what he's talking about. One cannot verify that the theology of the Berkeley messiah is supernaturally founded—that he has really gained special insights from his contact beings. His ideas, repulsively intriguing though they may be, may still just be *his* ideas, and not anything based on UFO communications. No one can know and not many people really care. But Geller is something else again. Many people would like to know how he does his thing. These same people would cite UFO contact or the like as the last possibility for explaining Geller, but they would nevertheless like to know.

Another Reality?

Serious scientists have been conducting non-publicized experiments with Geller, thinking that he may be the bridge between science and parapsychology. Others think he may be the missing answer to the UFO phenomena. Is there perhaps another kind of reality emerging that we are not accustomed to considering? Can a verifiable reason be found for Geller's unsettling performances?

Theoretical physicist Dr. Jack Starfatt called the results of the investigation "staggering" and said a new step had been taken in psychoenergetics, the study of mind energy. Dr. David Bohn, the eminent theoretical physicist, professor John Hasted of London University, and authors Arthur C. Clarke and Arthur Koestler were also involved in the research with Geller.[5]

The most extensive scientific experiments with Geller have been conducted over the past three years or so by Dr. Andrija Puharich, an Israeli physician and holder of fifty-six patents, who set out to understand the source of Geller's powers.[6] Puharich's book on the remarkable psychic is now on the stands. His experiments produced truly hair-raising results.

The doctor first eliminated the chance for any physically based hypotheses with carefully controlled experiments. Geller could routinely perform his astounding feats under rigidly restricted laboratory conditions.

Then, on December 1, 1971, the problem was "solved," or rather a strange new hypothesis developed. On that day, during a routine hypnosis experiment with Geller, Dr. Puharich heard a voice in the room, a disembodied speaker who announced himself as a representative of an extraterrestrial power.[7]

The experimenter devised a way to communicate with the voice and preserve the conversations. He placed a tape recorder on a table, which then began recording automatically. Dr. Puharich would question the "voice" and receive taped answers to his questions. When the coversation was finished, the doctor would transcribe the tape, and then the original would vanish.

Spectra Calling

With the cooperation of his mysterious visitors, Dr. Puharich has introduced other means of communication, such as the telephone, cables, TV, and radio (with regular broadcasting being interrupted).

Puharich dispassionately discusses the various classes of

beings that have communicated with him and Geller. The first group seems to have been in the nature of robot-computers with various identifying names like Rhombus 4-D, Spectra, etc. The voices imprinted on Puharich's tapes are similar to synthesized speech as produced by computers. A second group are creatures claiming to be humanoid in appearance and hailing from the planet Hoova, which they say exists outside our own Milky Way. Their recorded speech is like that of the human voice. Their lifespan, they say, is one million years. A third group consists of creatures yet to come: all the doctor can say is that they report that they are living beings from trillions of years hence! Lastly, there is a catch-all group who are very shy and won't identify themselves at all.

Dr. Puharich was told that the extraterrestrials from Hoova have been observing the earth for some 20,000 years. They have made contact with men sporadically during that time, they said. Some of their contactees were well known figures in world history. They always exacted a pledge of secrecy, but this apparently has been lifted in our time, as Dr. Puharich was asked to reveal their communications to mankind.

Geller performs his feats thanks to the advanced scientific knowledge of the planet Hoova, where all problems of life have been solved, say the voices. Their science encompasses transloca-tion of material objects, complete control over biological sys-tems, healing, the implantation of feelings and ideas into other minds, and the ability to travel across time as we travel across space.

Dr. Puharich says that the basic attitude of the extraterrestri-als is benevolent and that they wish to help mankind. Their superior knowledge can, of course, be beneficial to earthlings if we cooperate.

God Is an Idea

The occult connection seems apparent in the kinds of crea-tures given and their varied super-scientific abilities. Their being able to traverse time accounts for the ability of earthbound occultists to predict the future with fair accuracy. Assuming for a moment the presence of demons, it would be reasonable that a cunning demon would reveal a nugget or two about the future, or provide the abilities of one such as Uri Geller, in order to gain the confidence of the many. Demons, as we have seen from Scripture, do possess supernatural abilities, and they do use them to bad ends. That they put forth a benevolent image or lend their abilities for public relations purposes shows their shrewdness rather than their concern for us.

Sly remarks about God permeated the contact messages given Dr. Puharich: "The only way God can be reached is as an idea," and the like.[8] Some kind of anti-Christian theology is universally present in occult practices and most certainly present in the activites of demons.

Dr. Puharich, not to mention his intriguing subject, has been interested in the investigation of psychic phenomena for some time. His earlier pre-Geller works recount intensive examinations of several sensitives, including the famous medium Eileen Garrett and the Dutch occultist Peter Hurkos. Puharich was healed psychically by the Brazilian psychic surgeon Arigo,[9] and it was Arigo's death in 1971 that caused him to seek out Geller.[10]

Dr. Puharich's Masterpiece

Geller has been the doctor's masterpiece, surpassing the skills and the supernatural aura of any of the other subjects he has pursued. Since their first contact with the extraterrestrials together, Geller and Puharich have been consumed with the investigation and promotion of their discoveries. The extraterrestrials have said that they have plans for the intrepid psychic adventurers, and the two men have eagerly cooperated.

Geller was honored to hear from the extraterrestrials that he was the "only one to save mankind" and that he had been purposely given enormous powers.[12] He proceeded to achieve astral projection while under hypnosis by Puharich[13] and one time was apparently transported to another location. Eventually the extraterrestrials began telling the doctor *when* to hypnotize his clever subject so that they could speak through him.[14] Dr. Puharich learned that his old friend and mentor Arigo was still active, or, as the extraterrestrials stated through Geller, still "with them."[15]

Neither Geller nor Puharich is evil in the ordinary sense; rather, it seems, evil forces are perhaps able to work through them. The commentary of both men on the work they are doing is very revealing and shows two somewhat mystified human beings who are not entirely comfortable with all they are experiencing. They provide an interesting, wide-eyed commentary about their odd relationship with the aliens.

Both of them feel that these beings have abilities totally incomprehensible within the human experience. They think the extraterrestrials can take any physical shape they desire—from that of people to ants to UFO's. They believe that they can transport themselves anywhere in the universe and take the form of "matter-energy," which they say can be stored and recalled from various places in the world.[16] This would account for the more abstract UFO characteristics, such as vanishing and radar sightings.

Where they get their energy, of whatever form it is, is an open question. In seances the spirit seems to draw energy from the human host, typically leaving an exhausted medium after a contact. Geller feels the extraterrestrials utilize energy taken from his body. He experiences severe headaches at times of relative physical inactivity.[17]

Most significantly, these supposed extraterrestrials are eager to get their story told. They urged Puharich to write his book about Geller and to include in it everything about their activity and how information comes from them through Geller. Instructions are provided for novices to pursue the work of contacting, as was also true of Jane Roberts' book, *How to Develop Your ESP Powers.* Seth, dictating through his hostess, recommended several exercises for the development of ESP powers.

Hook or Hoax?

One gets the feeling, supposing demon activity again, that a scheme of entrapment is going on. In the manner of a dope pusher, they pass out samples to the unsuspecting. When the innocents get hooked, their allegiance is to the pusher.

Geller and Puharich together express an uneasy feeling about their whole experience, saying, in fact, that there is something "funny" or "wrong" about the situation. They cite a great many UFO's that only *they* can see. They wonder if they are being played with, whether the whole matter is just a big joke.[18] Several times the extraterrestrials have changed their "set and fixed" plans and done downright foolish things. Geller has wondered if they are unstable personalities despite their powers. At times he has feared that he is their slave and that they have no real concern for him or the world.[19]

All in all, the two don't act as if they are perpetrating a hoax, and in any case it has gained them little more than some attention, a goodly portion of it in the form of ridicule. Geller's astonishing powers are certainly real enough, or at least have been observed by reliable investigators.

Unlike Noonan, Geller doesn't seem perfectly satisfied with his position as a contact person nor with the behavior of his contacts, despite the extraordinary gifts they have reportedly provided him. The queasy feelings he expresses about the situation would be experienced by all of us in the same position. Undeniably, something exceedingly strange is going on in his life and it triggers a very natural averse reaction.

For our purposes, we see in the lives of Geller and his associate a distinct connection between occult phenomena and the UFO's. The contactees report that the extraterrestrials utilize UFO's and apparently travel in them. The major theory about UFO's, that they are vehicles carrying extraterrestrials, is satisfied by Geller's experiences and what he has been told.

Again, however, the demon theory is more embracing. We find it difficult to accept the popular "space travelers" theory because of the odd, occultish behavior of the UFO's, the seeming lack of a place for extraterrestrials to come from to begin with, and the religio-world control overtones so often associatiated with contact cases. Demons, on the other hand, do behave in the way UFO's behave, as we have said. They don't need a material place to come from and are most certainly interested in the world's theological future.

In any case, Uri Geller and his personal experimenter, Dr. Andrija Puharich, are alive and well and being examined carefully at present. We should be hearing more from them in the future.

The Voice of Interplanetary Parliament

Dr. George King mixes Yoga, "Christianity," and UFO's to come up with The Aetherius Society. Founded in August 1956, this cult was called by the *Los Angeles Times* "the most structured and perhaps the most explicitly religious of the UFO cults."[20]

King, born in England in 1919, received a command in 1954: "Prepare yourself! You are to become the Voice of Interplanetary Parliament."[21] He had been an accomplished practitioner in all forms of Yoga previous to this revelation. Eight days later he was visted by "a great master of Yoga" who was aware of the commandment. He had come to instruct King in advanced Yogic practices that would enable him to establish telepathic communication with a being from the planet Venus, a being called Aetherius.[22]

The devotee studied hard. In time he became adept at going into trance states and receiving the promised messages. The Society that was eventually founded now has branches in the United States, Europe, and Australia. Dr. King has enjoyed great success as an occult spiritual healer.[23] He has appeared on BBC television in England and KCOP-TV in Hollywood and has given hundreds of public demonstrations of his healing powers.

The group has undertaken "benevolent" acts through metaphysical ritual, some of which are difficult to explain except in the context of their theology. They performed Operation Prayer Power, designed to help in disaster situations; Operation Starlight, which "charged" nineteen mountains throughout the world with spiritual energy; Operation Blue Water, an attempt to develop the ability to place psychic energy directly into a "psychic center," i.e., strategic locations within the human body; Operation Sunbeam, a continual effort to "recharge" the earth (fourteen phases have been performed to date—required because of their belief that the earth is a living entity); and finally, Operation Karmalight, the transmitting of the evil entity Satan away from the earth. This last undertaking involved the occupation of material bodies by the cult's Three Adepts, or interplanetary beings. Needless to say, the effort to remove Satan has apparently not been successful, although it is doubtful that the cult's Satan is the Biblical Satan.

"Operation Prayer Power" gives a picture of an authentic spiritual effort, though actually the point was to store psychic energy. The Russians reportedly performed such an occult psychic energy-storage exercise to remove sludge from rivers and accomplish other tasks.[24] There is actually some efficacy to this technique, since, in the demon theory, it is supposed that any obeisance to the demons will be rewarded by help from them.

Yoga is labeled as demonic by Dr. Kurt Koch, who notes the occult powers of advanced Yoga-materialization, levitation, telekinesis, states of trance, the excursion of the soul, and many other spiritualistic phenomena.[25] A book exists called *Christian Yoga,* but the practice of Yoga is inseparable from its own non-Christian philosophy. Yoga is Eastern occultism in its very essence: Yoga texts are full of such warnings as death, insanity, and incurable illness resulting from misapplied Yoga techniques.[26]

The strange possession experience of King is reminiscent of the idea of a "sovereignty" operating in human life, as with the late Edgar Cayce of the Association for Research and Enlightenment. Taylor Caldwell, who was used to "prove" reincarnation to the public by hypnotic regression experiments, seems to be one of many other examples.[27] A kind of enlightenment apparently came to these people, which was then promoted vigorously despite its opposition to Christianity and the general world scheme of things.

King's Aetherius Society has as its main purpose the spreading of its teachings, and it gathers the crowd with its free-of-charge spiritual healing.[28] Dr. Koch feels that this healing is invalid as such; it merely transfers the disability from an organic to a psychic level "and so brings about an illness on a higher level."[29] One pictures a person healed in body but made sick in mind.

Overtones of the Antichrist are felt in the Aetherius philosophy, as with the gospel of Allen-Michael Noonan. The Society is at work preparing the way for the coming of the next Master—an alien who will be mightier than all of the earth's armies and who will "remove from the Earth" all those who don't heed his words.[30] There goes the purging of the "undesirables" again, seemingly always necessary for these various new orders!

The Cosmic Masters

In any case, the great Avatar (or Master) will eventually appear and "openly declare himself as the current Messiah."[31] Closer contact with extraterrestrials is encouraged by the Society, as is the reversing of the earth's "evil Karma." The extraterrestrials apparently don't care to land on the earth at this point because of all this evil Karma we have built up on our planet; but they will join us when the society and its advocates have done something about this.

A Brotherhood is to be formed based on the teachings of the Cosmic Masters. The basic beliefs of this order are a bit difficult to assimilate, mixing as they do some yogic philosophy, some Christian prophecy, and some UFO jargon into the bargain. We should keep in mind that these ideas, as listed below, come from "Aetherius" rather than King. He mouths the extraterrestrials' teachings, or so he reports.

Flying saucers, says the Society, are actually spacecraft from within our own solar system. Our own planets are classrooms from which we graduate in turn, progressing from one to the next in line. Jesus, Buddha, and Krishna came from Venus. The Bible refers in many places to flying saucers, King's followers say. The real spiritual heirarchy on earth is the Great White (for "white magic") Brotherhood, which is made up of Masters from all races. A great millennium is to appear, but not before universal turmoil and suffering have had their day.

Reincarnation is the backbone of this school of thought, and it is held to be nearly endless. Pantheism and Karma particularly, which "guarantees that eventually everyone will become a great spiritual being and will evolve back to God," are also part of the theology.

These and other teachings are allegedly received by Dr. King from Cosmic Masters from other planets while he is in his "positive Yogic Samadhic trance."[32] (Samadhic is defined as various grades of that state in which "the individual mind, freed for a time from all material limits, takes the form of supreme, omnipresent mind and gains enlightenment."[32])

Apparently the Society obtains quite a bit of information as King does his thing: they offer 27 books, 19 tapes, and 7 issues of *The Cosmic Voice* which includes their newsletter. They are definitely set up to promulgate what they consider to be the final word.

Another Gospel

Among the books offered by the Society is one ostensibly by Jesus. In some way King received new messages from Jesus which contradict those He gave originally! It's extremely difficult to even grasp the idea of the Lord renouncing His Gospel, but Dr. King's pronouncements unabashedly hazard this monstrosity.

The work is called *The Twelve Blessings* and was reportedly authored by Jesus Himself. In it the Lord is supposed to have said that there are many paths to God; what He had done in His earthly ministry was nothing—"not even worth of mention"—compared to the work of the Three Adepts (the interplanetary saviors). Jesus admits that He didn't really come to forgive our sins: the forgiving of sins is impossible in Karmic law. God is impersonal and "Law" personified, according to Jesus, in this version of theology. And finally, the Three Adepts are the true saviors of the world, "of every man, woman, child, animal, fish, tree, and rock upon the surface of this planet."[34]

A particularly heinous threat to the Society against its own adherents is that they must work to preserve their own salvation. The constant labor for the Three Adepts is instrumental in eventual deliverance, whatever that amounts to, and the greater reward goes to the more devoted worker. In that almost endless reincarnation is posited, one can expect to advance spiritually through one's lives, but if one does not help the movement right now, spiritual advancement is denied. In fact, one might not progress for another 287 lives in retribution for laziness at this particular point in time![35]

Spiritual advancement by the coming millennium is guaranteed to only a few. If we miss this opportunity to help Aetherius, we will "regret it for lives to come."[36] Only those who actively serve the Society can count on the final reward.

This "pidgin Christianity" reeks of the burden of discounting Biblical principles and undeifying the Savior. As in the case of the Allen-Michael Noonan doctrine, a certain amount of semi-accurate prophecy is slung into the works to give the whole business some class, but those discomfiting threats are always present.

Beyond the ever-present occultic practices and supernatural sources of the philosophy, it is this basic opposition to Christianity on the part of contactees that provides the simplest link to demons. The dependence on UFO's, or those who operate them, and the supposed existence of spirit beings who control our destiny, also sounds another familiar chord.

The Parallel World

To try to pull together the philosophies and theologies of Allen-Michael Noonan, Uri Geller, and George King, not to mention the thousands of other psychics to be found around the globe, is an impossible task. At first glance one is put off by what sound like the ravings of madmen; but then one has to reckon with the very real powers of such individuals, either to perform "miracles" of a kind or to influence followers so that their strange movements grow.

We have noted certain common features among the philosophies we have given, but the three psychics we have examined, even with their predilection toward UFO's, would make strange bedfellows. Noonan's coming world order doesn't seem a bit like the Eastern-flavored King's coming millennium; and these two in turn might well repulse the contacts who supply the impressive powers of Uri Geller.

But there is a bigger point to consider. What all of the occult practitioners, including the present three, do have in common is a sense of the spiritual. They are perverse believers in God's existence (or at least they mention Him freely), and they certainly believe in things supernatural. Geller even cites his queasy feelings about the whole matter and doesn't always seem eager to assume his assigned role as the world savior. Allen-Michael Noonan and George King surely believe that they are in contact with extraterrestrials; and indeed, their philosophical inventions seem well beyond the powers of ordinary spinners of tall tales.

It is high time that we all realize that there exists a spiritual—supernatural, invisible, whatever concept you prefer—world.

This world, not perceptible by our senses, moves along parallel to our earthly existence and affects us profoundly all the time. Essential matters vital to us all and yet not definable by natural or scientific means, like love, beauty, God, evil, ESP, and most likely UFO's, to mention a few, are all around us. We are aware of them only through their intrusion into our affairs, not by observation. But they *are* part and parcel of this human existence. More than that, they are the very essence of it.

This parallel world, as we are styling it, is a very full world, occupied by a variety of beings and entities, rather like the world we can see. The Bible characterizes the spiritual world as experiencing ongoing warfare on the angelic level—the very sons of God are in contention. We see it clearly in the painful experiences of Job, and we will see it objectively revealed in the Tribulation to come. The Book of Revelation presents quite a different world from that which we are accustomed to: in the end times of Revelation, the spiritual beings of good and evil will make themselves manifest on the earth, and there will be no further doubt as to what sort of conflict has been going on in their province.

Through the so-called Church Age, the time since Christ, the demons have been most subtle. God's Holy Spirit has been present on the earth, and the power of Christianity, the antidote to evil, has been available to all. The return of the Lord for His own is not very far off. And at this time, most expectedly, that parallel world, the province of the demons and the forces of good, is very restless. Christianity is realizing a tremendous revival; so is occultism and the forces of evil. So are UFOs.

The Sinister Revival

It will be considered as foolishness by some, but we feel that the explanation of the UFO's somehow fits into this revival. They are a manifestation of demon activity. They are here to misguide the multitudes and they are doing pretty well. They have judiciously utilized their powers through selected people to fascinate the masses, and they have widely promulgated their doctrines. They do not march through Times Square, of course, because this would reveal too much of the spiritual world. This might make people reconsider, as well, the existence of God, and the nether forces would have advertised for their enemy.

Are the flying machines really up there? Maybe so; it's not that important. If the demons wish them to be there, they are there, and if they wish people to imagine they're there, then they are imagined to be there. The spiritual world has very real control insofar as people choose a side in the conflict. If one has chosen Christ, one is not bothered by demons, or at least he is adequately armed against them. If one has chosen Geller or King or Noonan, et. al., then one is open to the powers behind them.

Are the demons "extraterrestrials?" Sure, in the sense that demons are not earth creatures at all. They have no material homes, just as they have no material existence. Are they just ideas of ours? No, not the way the Bible characterizes them. They have motives and they take action. We are by no means making them happen or just dreaming up their activities.

You can go on believing that there is no God, no occult practices that get valid results, no UFO's, no evil at work in the world (or good, for that matter), and nothing else that can't be objectively measured, such as love and beauty. But thinking people reject that. The presence of profoundly good and profoundly evil forces is intense in today's world, and any reasonably intelligent person knows it.

The danger is that if you refuse to accept the presence of this parallel world, it will simply engulf you. Prophecy sees a coming evil that will make all of our wars and all of our totalitarian regimes pale by comparison. You will be a part of the coming holocaust if you remain oblivious to its signs.

In Jesus' time people were more aware of possession and the occult. It was a different world—the one before the Church Age. Demons and angels were mentioned routinely in the Scriptures, and the dozens of pagan religions reckoned with them as a fact of life. When Jesus cast out demons, the crowds had their various opinions of the feats, but no one said that there were no demons to begin with.

When Jesus told them to test the spirits, they knew exactly what He meant. No one needed to ask Him what spirits were. But now, in the Age of Enlightenment, we scoff at the ideas of spirits. We just don't believe they exist and so we easily fall prey to them.

Satan's most masterful deception of the human race has come in these past few centuries before the return of Christ, and our impressive scientific advancement has fostered in us the conceit that we are the masters of the earth. Men became like gods because they perfected gadgets and made charts of evolution. They even acted like gods in selecting superior and inferior human strains, as with the Nazis. And Satan accomplished the awesome achievement of getting men to virtually forget about good and evil. We have become unconscious of God and unconscious of Satan. A few generations ago men were extremely conscious of the moral implications of what they did in this world, but now we laud the makers of vicious weapons and we stand awed by the practitioners of occult phenomena. It's now very chic to practice astrology and to be up on the lastest von Daniken tripe or to pronounce oneself a righteous atheist. We have made a primitive world indeed—one in which the superior killer survives as the ruler of the jungle.

Our science has given us the hydrogen bomb. Our worldly religious practice has given us a hopelessly false ecumenism. Our new morality has given us dope and illicit sex. And our increasing distance from our Creator has given the spirits around us the go-ahead to entertain us with deadly diversions.

We are intrigued with the magician and the psychic surgeon; we are hopeful about our morality; and we are passively curious about the strange flying objects in our airspaces. The UFOs are real—as real as this mad, ungodly world. Test the spirits!

FOOTNOTES

1. Dr. Andrija Puharich, *Uri* (New York: Anchor, 1974), p. 134.
2. Puharich, "Uri Geller and Extraterrestrials," in *Psychic* May-June 1974, pp. 13-16; Blum, p. 225.
3. June 1974, pp. 46, 48.
4. *Psychic,* pp. 16-17, note 2.
5. *National Enquirer,* Oct. 7, 1974. See also a recent *Nature* article for the SRI investigations.
6. Puharich, *Uri* (New York: Bantam, 1975) p. 249.
7. Puharich, *Uri; Psychic,* p. 16, note 2.
8. See *Uri,* Bantam Edition, Appendix 1, for distinctly unbiblical views.
9. Puharich, *Uri,* Anchor Edition, pp. 25-35.
10. Ibid., p. 7.
11. Ibid., pp. 94-95.
12. Ibid., p. 100.

13. Ibid., pp. 99-100.
14. Ibid., p. 125.
15. Blum, p. 151.
16. Puharich, *Uri,* Anchor Edition, pp. 126-127, 152, 171.
17. Ibid., p. 208.
18. Ibid., p. 173.
19. Ibid., pp. 188-189.
20. *Los Angeles Times,* Sept. 8, 1974.
21. Tract from the Society: "A Brief Introduction."
22. Ibid.
23. Note 20 and tract "You are Responsible" from The Society.
24. On the idea of stored psychic energy see Puharich, *Uri,* p. 92.
25. Kurt Koch, *The Devils Alphabet* (Kregel, 1969), p. 126; Rummurti S. Mishra, *Fundamentals of Yoga* (Doubleday-Anchor, 1974), p. 151.
26. Hans-Ulrich Rieker, *The Yoga of Light,* (Dawn Horse Press), pp. 9, 133-134, 15, 20, 31, 52, 81; Ernest Wood, *Seven Schools of Yoga* (Wheaton: Wuest & Theosophical Publishing Company), pp. 14, 78-79, 84; Mircea Eliade, *Yoga Immortality and Freedom* (Princeton; Princeton Univ. Press, 1971), pp. 95-100, 40, 35; E. Wood, *Yoga* (Baltimore: penguine, 1971), p. 173; R. S. Mishra, *Fundamentals of Yoga* pp. 4, 34, 42, 31, 80-82; G. Miller Feuerstein, *Yoga and Beyond* (New York: Schocken 1972), pp. 7, 28, 34. On Yoga being inseparable from its theory, see Mishra, pp. 1, 4, 5, 182-184, 189; Eliade, pp. 3, 38; Wood, *Seven Schools of Yoga,* pp. 23, 25; Pantanjalis Yoga Aphorisms 1:7; 1:29; P. Yogananda, *Autobiography of a Yogi,* pp. 264-266.
27. A study of the lives of these individuals shows this clearly. This is probably true for most occultists.
28. Tract, "A Brief Introduction."
29. Kurt Koch, *Christian Counseling and Occultism* (Kregel, 1972), p. 192; M. Unger, *Demons in the World Today,* "Healing" chapter.
30. Tract, "Some Basic Principles."
31. *Los Angeles Times,* Sept. 8, 1974.
32. Tract, "Some Basic Principles."
33. R. S. Mishra, *Fundamentals of Yoga* (Anchor, 1974), p. 206.
34. G. King, *The Three Saviours Are Here,* pp. 12-15, 21-25.
35. Ibid., pp. 30, 48.
36. Ibid., p. 29

Ufology should rightfully be a branch of psycical research.

John A. Keel
Merseyside UFO Bulletin
Sept. 1970

We can consequently conclude that it is impossible to interpret the UFO phenomena in terms of material spaceships as we conceive of the latter, i.e. in terms of manufactured self-propelled machines retaining their material nature and their mechanical structure to travel from one solar system to another by traversing the distance separating these systems in the Einstein-ian continuum.

Physicist Dr. Jacques Lemaitre
Flying Saucer Review
Vol. 14, No. 6

To summarize: neither a crash program staffed with twenty Nobel prize winners, nor computer correla-tions of millions of poorly observed parameters, nor mental telepathy with superior space beings, nor the organization of hundreds of people into observation squads, scanning the heavens every night with binocu-lars and a pure heart, will easily dispose of a problem that has eluded our radar, aircraft, astronomers and physical theories for so long. . . . I cannot offer the key to this mystery. I can only repeat: the search may be futile; the solution may be forever beyond our grasp; the apparent logic of our most elementary deductions may evaporate."

Jacques Vallee
Passport To Magonia

Beliefs and theories; imagination and dream and pre-tension; tormented human souls, trying to reach for their small infinite, fancy they catch a star. In a forest of theories each man climbs his own tree. He reigns on his branch and directs insults at the mockingbird. Undisturbed, lines of facts stretch across the horizon with patience. But night falls on the scene, and men go to sleep. In this night they remain, unidentified in their relative universe. A hand from Heaven reaches down into their dreams, and they wonder.

Jacque Vallee
UFO's in Space

After more than twenty years' association with the (UFO) problem, I still have few answers and no viable hypothesis.

J. Allen Hynek,
The UFO Experience, Epilogue

8

Let Us Take You
To Our Leader

We realize that this is a book of puzzles, with its talk of UFO's, ESP, saviors, demons, extraterrestrials, cosmic leaders, and on and on. But, as in all good puzzle books, the answers are in the back. We believe we have the answers—or *the* answer—and we would be remiss not to present it. We think it's the only way to go, in view of all that's happening in this failing world of ours. But first, let's review the puzzles.

The Puzzles

We began with the query, "What on earth is going on?" and we declared that the UFOs are real. From our point of view they're as real as the rise of occultism or the revival of Christianity. They're as real as the strange changes in our climate, the environmental deterioration of Planet Earth, as real as hunger, inflation, apostasy, and the whole discouraging human condition.

We pointed out, for the benefit of those who don't know, that UFO sightings have become increasingly common throughout the world and that several governments have discrete plans for investigating them. We noted that books like those of von

Daniken enjoy an enormous following and that interest in the stranger theories of man and his history are in vogue today. We quoted surveys that indicate a tremendous interest in UFO's on the part of Americans, with fifteen million of us claiming to have seen one and fifty-one percent of those surveyed saying that they believe the UFO's are real.

We told of government panels examining the evidence and coming out with guarded statements implying that if the UFO's were really there they weren't worth bothering about. But we also cited the interest of senators, astronauts, pilots (like those who patrol the White House airspace), and scientists of integrity. We cited a huge variety of "explanations" of our uninvited guests of the airways, ranging from the popular extraterrestrial - visitors theory to the unsettling non-material craft theories.

The apparently hostile nature of the UFO's was evidenced in any number of reported cases coming from sources of varied repute—from flying saucer magazines to cautious UFO study organizations to U.S. Government files. We have patiently reviewed "contactee" reports, and we certified that there exist thousands of such testimonies. We noted that the U.S. government classified a particularly embarrassing case involving extraterrestrial contact with trusted personnel of the Intelligence services. The material remained secret for some fifteen years, only recently having released, conceivably in connection with the new "hang-out" policy demonstrated by the TV Special.

We discussed the idea of a coming Age of Aquarius, taking into account that large numbers of spiritual disciplines, including Christianity, are expecting big changes in the near future. Many of the cults speak of a rather threatening time to come, but one resulting in ultimate benevolence—a concept not out-of-line with the Biblical view. We drew strict differences, however, between the interpretations as we tested the spirits. A great many of the cults, and Christianity too, we felt, associate the UFO's with the coming big changes.

We dug into the past to some degree, finding UFO-style reports in certain ancient sources, with indications of mysterious goings-on in the skies. Written records of sightings during the Middle Ages are fairly common and often strikingly similar to today's reports. Astronomers, explorers like Christopher Columbus, and early scientists of the Age of Enlightenment were apparently puzzled by sightings, as were theologians who founded occult-based sects. Philosphers and Bible critics came up with a great deal of secular thought based on man being wholly in charge of his own destiny, while the UFO's apparently conducted business as usual over their heads.

We noted the propensity of the UFO's to keep up with the scientific Joneses, seemingly becoming more complex as man grew more capable of describing them. Whole fleets came on the scene as well as huge airships, but always the UFO's kept a step ahead of man's ability to apprehend them.

The twentieth century brought the ghost fliers and all of the mischief of daredevil flight navigation over the Swedish mountains. World War II saw no letup as the UFO's followed the action with abandon, being spotted repeatedly at the wingtips of planes on both sides of the battle.

Finally the saucers and discs of the modern era of UFO's came on the scene to stay, apparently. The White House was buzzed repeatedly, along with weapons installations. Pursuit seemed hopeless, but radar verified the presence and flight patterns of the elusive craft. The U.S. Air Technical Intelligence Center carried on a fruitless vendetta against the wily enemy above. Government projects were started and stopped. All sorts of reliable observers started to see UFO's, and experienced airmen began to clock their speeds and their unbelievable maneuverability.

A "cover-up" was undertaken and penalties were assigned for those reporting sightings in the armed services. But reports from civilians continued to pour in and the cover-up has now apparently been lifted.

Recapping the Evidence

"UFO's—Do you Believe?" the December 15, 1974, TV Special, was a landmark in the public reportage of UFO phenomena. The documentary gave its evidence plainly, showing a cross-section of witnesses to UFO's and offering the data to the viewer noncommittally, as its title suggested. The Defense Department apparently cooperated in the effort, and the substantial UFO files stored at Maxwell Air Force Base were shown on screen. It was stated, deadpan, that the Air Force had recorded 12,618 individual sightings in those files. Soldiers, a policeman, a farmer, an astronaut—surely, a fair representation of American citizenry—took their turns describing their sightings.

The infamous Pascagoula abduction was given a thorough going-over, with the two participants and many of those who had examined them appearing to testify. It certainly did not appear that the documentary meant to discredit their story. The Special concluded with the announcer's very unique statement, "We have a real and persistent phenomenon. . . ."

We attempted to make the information on sightings "add up," but like everyone else we were stymied, scientifically speaking. The best we could say is that the UFO's are here to drive us crazy with unanswered questions.

We pursued the interplanetary visitors theory but found some difficulty with the existence of outer-space planets to begin with, let alone visitation by their populace. We ran into problems with the hypothetical planets having to experience a hypothetical spontaneous generation and then having to experience a hypothetical evolution in order to have any sort of life at all. And then we have our troubles trying to assume that this doubly hypothetical life would be advanced, humanoid, and interested in us. (See appendix: Life By Chance In Outer Space?)

We ended up referring to Dr. George G. Simpson, a Harvard professor, who didn't like the odds at all. He rated the chances of all these probabilities happening in the sequence and manner desired as "not significantly greater than zero." Professor of Chemistry Donald England concluded, "Any speculation as to imaginary men on imaginary planets is pure idle speculation."

We wondered if the UFO's came from our own solar system planets and might be "in the family," sharing our sun. But the facts look very discouraging there, also. Our probes have turned up nothing like life in our solar system, and liquid water, seemingly essential to life as we know it, is found only on the earth in this particular solar system.

We went into the "unscientific method," looking for clues in the behavior of the UFO's which might suggest their origin or purpose. But their behavior brings up more headaches than answers. They refuse to behave the way they *should* behave. Around here we just don't operate aircraft at supersonic speeds and low altitudes, making ninety-degree turns, to say nothing of fooling around with the inviolate laws of mechanics and propulsion. The punishment for an earthling trying to do with a flying machine what these UFO's are doing would be swift and final.

Then we have their reported propensity for changing shape and color, and their confounding antics, which suggest a superior race of utter goof-offs rather than serious scientists. We fall into the position of Uri Geller with his occult contacts—we're mightily impressed by their skills, but deeply disappointed in their carryings-on.

We ultimately concluded that little in our science and little in their behavior gave a clue about the UFO's. They just won't classify in either of those ways.

We then resorted to consulting the folks who know them— Allen-Michael Noonan and company, to begin with. The Berkeley messiah claims a close cameraderie with the UFO set, from whom he received his prophetical doctrine. We found the doctrine both distasteful and partially true. Noonan's view of a coming new world order and his utilization of the terms and concepts of Revelation give us the eerie feeling that he really does know something, or has learned something from sources quite superior to ones ordinarily available. Were he a Bible believer, we would say that he is aware of some prophecy but has perverted it in its future application. Since he certainly *isn't* a believer, we get the idea that he is really being coached as he says he is.

We noted the work of supernatural beings in the life of Job, and the general abilities of angels, fallen and unfallen, as they appear in the Bible. We indicated that serious Bible students have little trouble believing that Allen-Michael knows a thing or two. What they justly suspect are his motives.

We noted particularly his coming "passive" revolution and how it will rid us of the "undesirables" who oppose his world unity plans (or the plans of his UFO-borne coaches).

Taking off from the conviction of Noonan's disciples that "the occult circles had the greater truths all along," we examined in detail modern occult practices. We found that the occult has crept into the newspapers, bookshelves, scientific laboratories, doctors' offices, and myriad other sectors of daily modern life. An up-to-date occult sophisticate may obtain his future from an astrological column, check out the latest news from the extraterrestrials through a book by a contactee, test his own ESP at a university-supported lab, heal his aches and pains by a visit to a psychic surgeon, and finally make his own contact with the spirit world through any number of operating cults. He may reach the spirits on his own with a ouija board, in his dreams, or through a serious training effort complete with exercises to develop his capacity for relating with the demons.

We might take a moment to emphasize how much this occult connection has increased of late. Only a generation ago such goings-on were for a few weirdos, with the skeptics laughing up their sleeves. Now an increasing number, to judge from book sales, astrological popularity, and so forth, are dabbling in the occult. What we now experience routinely as a part of modern life was the science fiction of yesterday.

Noting the correlation between occult phenomena and the reported UFO phenomena, we investigated many contactee claims. Historically, and up to the present, many people have claimed a relationship with nether forces, with certain similarities to their reports. We looked into the practice of magic and the phenomenon of possession, through which many gain occult information.

We discovered that the occult connection presents the first hint of a system or logic to the activities of UFO's, since the two phenomena seem to have so much in common. We examined the study of Captain Ivar Mackay of the British UFO Research Organization, who is one of several convinced that there is an important relationship between UFO's and the occult.

And finally, in the previous chapter, we looked at the lives of two "occult celebrities" who claim constant contact with UFO operators and who have gained significant followings. Uri Geller's relationship with his space contacts and George King's incredible extraterrestrial communication through the powers of Yoga may have surprised some readers who were not aware of the utter dedication and the very effective powers of such devotees. Their activities led us to serious consideration of what we call "the parallel world."

This parallel world is, in effect, the place where the spirits live—both good and evil. Should we be seriously considering "spirits"? Does anybody have a better idea?

The Answers

We are now ready to look at demons—the *how,* the *why,* and the *what.* We think the occult connection holds the answers to all of our puzzles.

Obviously there really is very little we can say about just how demons make people see UFO's, but we do know something, these days, about the human brain and how it works (and how it can be *made* to work). In the thirties it was suggested that brain activity was electric; today we know this to be true. We now utilize an electroencephalograph machine (EEG) to record brain activity, and we have classified certain electrical rhythms which we associate with various mental activities. The Alpha state, for example, is known to be concerned with vision.

We know, too, that via special chemical activity, nerve cells conduct electrical impulses in the brain. There are an estimated ten billion nerve cells in the human brain which play a key role in emotional responses and sensations. At any given moment billions upon billions of electrical impulses are being carried through the nerve cells, and all of our perceptions and impressions of the world around us are intimately connected with this phenomenon.

The brain is indeed a wonderful machine and very adequately adapted to perceiving what we need to know of our environment. But most important for our consideration here is the discovery of how one might interfere with the normal workings of the brain and produce paranormal results. Drugs like the hallucinogens affect the perceptions of the brain, and electrical impulses induced synthetically produce false impressions of reality. It is theoretically possible to cause almost any sort of perception by inducing the appropriate impulse into the brain. Hallucinations, visions, and even emotional experiences might be caused synthetically—even whole sequences of imaginary events!

Simple hypnotism is a routine example of how the brain may be induced to render false perceptions. The dentist drills in the tooth of a patient who has been persuaded that he will experience a feeling of well-being and encounter no pain. Or the audience chuckles in a night club as the hypnotist convinces his volunteer from the crowd that he is taking a shower onstage.

Those exercises are beneficent, or at least innocuous, but the point that the brain is not a reliable perceiver under certain induced circumstances is something to think about in connection with our investigation. If reality may be "manipulated," anything can happen (or be reported to have happened).

Another instance in which the brain is not reliable is in the presence of phenomena it is not equipped to perceive. The air is full of TV and radio programs, electric and magnetic fields, and so forth, but the brain is not "tuned" to perceive them. To perceive TV waves we have to have a special receiver, thankfully. Our heads would be cluttered with an inconceivable burden of information about our environment if the brain were not designed to receive messages selectively. Of course we still perceive everything we want to know about the world whether or not we're afraid to ask.

Who Turned Out the Lights?

Magnetic fields are particularly relevant to our discussion because they are associated with UFO's. The UFO's give off strong enough fields to alter electric current in the vicinity, and this fact is conceivably behind the reported failures of auto electrical systems, radar, airplane ignitions systems, etc. The Russians tried to fire on a squadron of UFO's hovering over a Moscow defense network, but with little luck. Their first two salvos, fired by experts, exploded in flight short of their target. The third salvo didn't get off the ground—the electric circuitry of the whole missile base had failed![2]

A good deal of research has been carried out on the effect of fluctuating magnetic fields on the brain. They have produced such effects as visual sensations and certain mental affects.[3] Experimenter Maxwell Cade, a specialist in radiation medicine, electronics, and astronomy, demonstrated that UFO's and "ghosts" could be experienced as real when electromagnetic fields were focused on the human brain. He said evidence exists for both "subjective impressions and objective psychological changes" that were produced or set off by electromagnetic radiation of a certain range.[4]

Uri Geller is virtually one big walking magnetic field. When he was tested at the Stanford Research Institute on a magneto-meter, an instrument which measures the strength of magnetic fields, the results were deemed "impossible." The strength of Geller's personal magnetic field reached the top of the instru-ment's scale, or three-tenths of a gauss. According to the Stan-ford Research Institute, Geller's strength is "a significant mag-netic field," comparable to that of the earth's.[5]

Geller also drives Geiger counters wacky. The normal back-ground rate is one count per second, but Geller drew up to 150 per second! He's a strange one in many ways.

Phosphenes are visual sensations produced by means other than light, usually alternating magnetic currents. The optic nerve, it has been found, can be stimulated without light actual-ly falling on the retina. Obviously, false visual images are pro-duced. We might liken this to the "beams" that hit observers from UFO craft. Though they are usually described as beams of light, they could conceivably be beams of magnetic current.

At least one authority has considered that an intense mag-netic field could be localized and shot at a human brain, thus producing all sorts of false perceptions.[6] All this opens up new light on the "contactee" cases. Where the more normal type of sightings are concerned, the ability to project an image is cer-tainly a possibility, considering the powers of demons. The UFO's could even be the demons themselves or temporary manipulations of matter and energy.[7]

This kind of reasoning really expands the enigmas, to say the least. We are quite accustomed to the idea of a good storyteller causing us to visualize what he's relating or of being given an emotional lift by a fine work of art. But the manipulation of magnetic fields to confuse our normal response patterns and make us believe what simply is not there is quite another bag of tricks. And that, of course, is what we think it is.

We believe demons can induce a whole series of experiences that, in fact, never really happened, similar to the experiences Uri Geller and Dr. Puharich found were induced by their extraterrestrial contacts.[8] They can also, however, through various means produce "real" UFO's which are visible to anyone. The demons in the Bible could literally manipulate and transform matter (Exodus 7:9-12; 22:8:7), and many psychics have shown similar powers through the help of evil spirits. Thus, with the powers we know demons have, they could *theoretically* transform a large chunk of rock into a UFO, assume human form inside of it, and land openly, thus "proving" the existence of advanced intergalactic civilizations. More likely, however, the valid UFO sighting is either a projection into our atmosphere, a temporary manipulation of matter and energy on a reduced level, or the self-transformation of whatever "material" the demons themselves are composed of.

To make a long story short, we think the demons are utilizing this property of magnetic fields, or some other phenomenon we as yet know nothing about, to affect the perceptions of those who see or contact them.

Yet how do we know demons, or anything else for that matter, are behind all these false projections and perceptions? Maybe magnetic fields are just running amuck by themselves. Maybe people are driven "out of focus" and they tend to see what the imaginings of their times might suggest—strange flying machines and visitors from outer space. Have the UFO's given us anything that shows intelligence behind it? Is there anything at all objective in their behavior? Consider the following case.

Betty Hill's Stars

In 1961 Betty and Barney Hill were allegedly taken aboard a UFO. Betty hit it off with the crew captain and he showed her a star map of trade routes and exploration paths involving a certain grouping of stars.[9]

Betty and Barney were released unharmed, but they both

began to experience nightmares. This condition continued for some three years until they consulted Boston psychiatrist and neurologist Dr. Benjamin Simon. Dr. Simon undertook time-regression hypnosis in order to have the Hill's relive their unsettling abduction.

Under post-hypnotic suggestion Betty was able to reproduce the star map she allegedly was shown on the space craft. That was in 1964. No one knew what to make of the map with its twenty-seven stars, because a certain pattern of three of the stars was unknown at that time and the other twenty-four were difficult to place in the universe with known materials. It was easily assumed that Mrs. Hill simply had a vivid imagination.

Then they started finding the stars!

In 1969, after five years of work, MUFON Field Investigator and Research Specialist Marjorie Fish found nine of the main stars, correlating them to a known pattern in the Constellation Reticulum. By 1972 just the three mysterious stars were mssing. Finally they too were discovered as a triangle of background stars (Giliese numbers 86.1, 95, 97).[10] Without the updated Giliese Catalogue of Nearby Stars released in late 1969 these final three stars could never have been found.

It was conceded that no astronomer could have drawn so accurate a star map as Betty Hill's in 1964. Miss Fish says that "only contact with extraterrestrials" could have produced that map. The rather conservative Aerial Phenomena Research Organization call's Miss Fish's monumental task of identifying the star pattern "one of the most important accomplishments" in UFO research.[11] The MUFON 1974 Symposium, pp. 69-80, gives more extensive evidence concerning the map and the fact that it cannot have been a hoax.

What are we to make of the case? If Betty Hill had a hallucination and saw a UFO and its crew, she would be just another abductee with another tale of extraterrestrials. But this housewife mapped stars no astronomer had found. Where did she get that information? Or better, *who* gave it to her?

The case suggests that the demons are certainly not trying to hide. That they have revealed themselves in other connections, through sightings, airplane encounters, occult contacts, and so forth we have already seen. But they have always just given us "philosophy," or some sort of dogma that men might well dream up on their own, though most of it, as we saw, did seem beyond the powers of its purveyors. With Geller they gave us demonstrations of inexplicable ESP powers, but that sets us to examining Geller to see if he is not just a clever magician.

Betty Hill's map is something else again. It exists, it's quite correct, and it's just impossible that Betty Hill or anybody else on this earth could have produced it in 1964. Why are they tipping their hand like that? Why are they revealing that they really are supernatural creatures? What's in it for them?

Let us consider briefly the magnitude of the UFO phenomenon. It is historical in its context and worldwide in its magnitude. It has increased dramatically in the last few years, both in interest, research, and sightings. A computer analysis of nearly fifty thousand UFO sightings over the last twenty-seven years has revealed definite patterns of behavior. There seems to be increased activity every sixty-one months. Every five years and one month they have been moving across the globe from west to east in 1500 to 2000 mile leaps. Sightings during these peak periods range from ten to one-hundred times the normal number.[12] With such a compendium of sightings confronting us, wouldn't it be natural to conclude that they seem to be very deliberately revealing themselves to the whole earth so that we would be left with little choice but to believe what we're seeing?

The Coming Invasion

Quite simply, we think the demons are preparing the coming of the Antichrist.

In a way, we agree with Noonan and the others—there *is* a new world order coming (two, in fact), and the Christians are not at all part of the plan. This world is shortly to experience what Bible students call the Great Tribulation. After that, Jesus Christ will return to establish His millennial kingdom, in which at last God's will shall be done in earth as it is in heaven.

The Great Tribulation is to last seven years, during which time this world will see the full wrath of God. The Christians will be gone, as Noonan indicated, but certainly not killed out by a radio weapon. The Rapture of the Church will have occurred before the Great Tribulation; the Lord will have come for His people, as He said he would. In those terrible seven years, the Antichrist will be the world ruler, and his dictatorship will proceed headlong into Armageddon, that last great war.

The Antichrist is not your run-of-the-mill world dictator. He is, in fact, something we have never contended with before:

> He is a political leader of great acumen—virtually a sorcerer. He is engaging and appealing. He captures the loyalty of what is left of the world after the rapture, and he becomes a kind of inverse messiah. The world trusts him with its problems, and he certainly succeeds in putting it out of its misery. . . .
> He does demonstrate seemingly supernatural powers, but they are not from above. The best that can be said of him is "the devil made him do it."[13]

Here's where we think the UFO's come in. To properly set the stage for the Antichrist, who really is a supernatural personality, the world has to be made ready to think in terms of the new and the strange. This is evidenced in both Dr. Carl Jung's and Jacques Vallee's concern that UFO phenomena is producing specific changes in the collective psyche of mankind. The world has lost hope of some man ever coming forth out of one of the nations and solving its myriad problems. But some "non-man" stepping out of what is supposed to be a greatly superior civilization somewhere out in space—now that's real help! While this idea is speculative, we feel the possibility does need to be presented. Among other things, it would explain why the demons have gone to so much trouble. Also, since the UFO phenomenon is of a parapsychological nature, massive new research of UFO's would, in effect, help set up the scientific study of occultism, possibly on a worldwide basis. A third possibility is that the Antichrist will bring about a world unification through man's need to combine forces against a common enemy—in this case, hostile invaders from other worlds.

It is evident that if there are now several thousand documented cases of UFO landings, a type of "invasion" is already underway, even though the landings are not what we would classify as open or even well acknowledged.

It is the authors belief however that the UFO sightings and landings will continue to increase to the extent that it will be more clearly recognized that an "invasion" is indeed taking place. Whether this will eventually involve the open and highly publicized physical landing of craft with occupants, the materialization of beings *claiming* to be extraterrestials, or some other aspect, only time will tell. However, these "secret" landings could be preparatory for more open landings and bolder actions later on. This would again allow for the existence of demons upon the earth in materialized form. Many contactees report the extraterrestrials say *they will appear in a visible, tangible form upon the earth.* Many occultists report similar expectations for "ascended Masters" or "exalted Beings." Remember also that the anti-Christ, *himself,* would not have to be extraterrestrial. He could easily be of human birth, yet controlled (or possessed) by a *supra-physical* entity from some greatly advanced planet or dimension in space. Whether these beings, (if they appear as they say they will) will come as our friendly brothers from space, anxious to help man set up a one-world government of peace and harmony, or as evil entities to be united against, also remains to be seen. One thing is certain. Large endeavors encompass large plans. The UFOs should be up to something big. Several popular authors who write on UFO related topics have received their information via occult means (Charroux from "exalted beings", Von Daniken from astral projection into the past, Drake from a psychic, etc.) They all refer to man being the product of breeding experiments by extraterrestrials thousands of years ago. (If this were true, we could expect them to return to us. After all we are *their* product.) Dr. Vyacheslov Zaitzev, addressing a Russian parapsychology meeting stated: "If we really were visited centuries ago, we may be on the threshold of a 'second coming' of intelligent beings from outer space."[14] There are a number of ufologists and scientists who also think this is a possible event. And Dr. Jung believes UFOs may be preparing the world for significant changes which will catch some unprepared.[15] Also, if the large number of reported disappearances in connection with UFOs and the Bermuda Triangle are valid, this may in effect be preparing the world to accept the rapture.

Also, implicit in all UFO performances is the thought that Jesus is not the answer, or not the *only* answer. After all, if there really is a successful civilization out there, then the Bible with its earthbound ideas looks rather provincial, and the oldtime religion must bow to something as new and exciting as outer-space technology. Yet the Bible itself questions this idea: "Indeed, ask now concerning the former days which were before you, since the day that God created man on the earth, and inquire from one end of the heavens to the other. Has anything been done like this great thing, or has anything been heard like it? (Deut. 4:32 see context)

If, as the UFO folks imply, there are billions of inhabited planets out there with their variety of craft and their interplanetary organizations, Jesus' sacrifice looks rather paltry. If He really were to die for *all* of God's creatures, assuming we're acknowledging the existence of God, He'd have to die billions of times, in billions of forms, and so forth. It would make the Gospel look ridiculously inadequate. If these extraterrestrials are unfallen, then they certainly should not oppose the Biblical view of Christ. (See appendix: The Bible and Life In Outer Space).

Interstellar Apostasy

So the demons are pulling off a double-header of apostasy with the UFO program. They set the stage for a supernatural, or at least an extraterrestrial, solution for world problems; and then they attack the credence of the Scriptures, the true solution. We'll have to hand it to Satan. He's still the most subtle beast of the field.

People really *are* crying out for a world leader right now. God knows we need one, and the extraterrestrials know it too. They will be willing to help out. After all, aren't we all brothers in the same universe, and don't they have an organization of planets?

Of course there will be a price to pay. They'll be glad to send a representative, but he shouldn't have to put up with dissidents when he has only come to help. The undesirable elements will be removed in a miraculous way and everybody will be happy. We shouldn't be bothered by this unfortunate necessity, as Noonan has already told us, since it's for the greater good in the end.

The coming world leader would be virtually worshipped as God on the earth. We know that he will finally proclaim himself as such. The Bible details that one-of-a-kind blasphemy that starts the world toward Armageddon. His ideas will work for a while too, no doubt because he will have the cooperation of whatever governments and religions exist at the time. Also, if Uri Geller can bend steel bars with mind-over-matter, we can imagine the talents of his instructors' teacher! This Antichrist will at least fascinate people, even while he arranges their collective demise.

It should be appreciated that today's prophetic events, like the end-time prophecies we've been discussing, are less a matter of faith than of evidence. As we have seen, the Scriptures comment accurately on the state of affairs in today's world. Concrete predictions of the prophets, such as the restoration of Israel, the common market, world ecumenism, famine, and a host of others are present in the world right now, and they implicitly announce the end.

As always, there are only two great forces at work today—God and Satan—and the middle ground is disappearing. It's time now to make a choice.

The Truth Will Set You Free

Normally, in a book authored by a believer, you can find some evangelistic effort at its conclusion—some reference to making one's peace with God, receiving Christ, getting one's life on a solid spiritual footing, etc. This book is no exception, but in our context the evangelism is very simple. We need not preach a lengthy gospel, discuss your behavior, or compare doctrines. The way things stand today, the matter of spiritual allegiance boils down to this: you're about to be enslaved, but the Truth will set you free.

We've spoken of so many strange and supernatural matters in this book that no one should have his credulity strained if we mention God. We think He's real and He's there; we think He knows all about UFO's and all about us, His handiwork.

When Job was putting up with the best Satan had to offer, God stood by him and Job's faith held out. He received a great reward from God by keeping a clear mind in the face of a supernatural adversary. Obviously we have the same challenge today. All of us face the test of Job.

Unlike the demons of the UFO's, God does not require you to make special preparations to be a member of His kingdom. You need have no special talents or abilities. Jesus, as God on earth, turned no one away. In fact, He sought out the meek and the poor in spirit and promised them the universe.

You don't have to be religious. Jesus chose disciples from secular trades whose collective theological knowledge would have impressed no one. You don't have to be good. He came to the bad, He said. Didn't He take the thief hanging beside Him to Paradise with Him?

Know this, that when you line up with God you will be joining a society at least as exciting, forward-looking, and world-changing as any the demons inspire. And you will no longer be prey to every new idea that comes along in this panicky world. You'll have the mind of Christ operating within, and you need fear nothing.

Coming to Christ is as simple as asking—so just ask. He's listening.

But remember—so are *they*, up there in their UFO's. Don't be afraid to tell them what you think.

Receiving Christ

Coming to know Christ personally is the easiest and most rewarding thing that can ever happen to you. If you aren't certain that you have personally accepted Jesus Christ into your life, then you should do so right now. You don't have to know a lot about theology. You don't have to be good or moral. You don't have to have a lot of faith. In fact, all you need is an honest desire to receive Jesus Christ into your life. By bearing the judgment of a Holy God that was due your sins, Christ opened up the way for you to enter into a new relationship with God. In fact, it was God's great love for you that sent Jesus to the cross. He offers you new life now, and eternal life to come—a life that is far above our present life in beauty, challenge, joy and perfection. It is up to you to change your destiny. Jesus said, "Behold, I stand at the door (of your heart) and knock, if anyone hears My voice and opens the door, I will come into him, and will dine (have fellowship) with him, and he with Me" (Revelation 3:20 NASB).

Right now, in your own way, you can thank Jesus for dying for your sins and invite Him to come into your life. You have everything to gain and nothing to lose. If you would accept the gift of a friend, how much more should you accept the Love of God—a gift of everlasting life? Right now, why don't you put this book aside and come to know the God who loved you enough to sacrifice His only Son in your behalf? Thank Him that Christ has died for your sins and invite Jesus Christ into your life.

If you just received Christ, we want to be the first to welcome you into God's family! Jesus Christ is now living inside you and He has promised, "I will never desert you, nor will I ever forsake you" (Hebrews 13:5 NASB). You have a God and a friend, for life—forever.

There are a few helpful principles that will encourage you in you new relationship with Christ. The first thing is to realize that God knows you fully—he knows everything there is to know about you—and he still loves and accepts you just as you are. Secondly, since He loves you, He wants the best for you —to change your desires about life to His desires. He will guide us in this as we make ourselves available to His Spirit, who now lives in us. As we learn to trust Christ, He will begin to produce in us a new love for God and others. Our life will grow richer and more rewarding. This is a process, however, that takes time so don't get discouraged. To be honest, you can expect to have some ups and downs, but God will continually prove His faithfulness to you. Third, the best way you can deepen your relationship to God is to read His Word, and the Gospel of John is a good place to start. Ask Christ to teach you as you study and He will. Fellowship with other believers in Christ will also be helpful. Never forget that you are now a child of God (I John 3:1) and that He will never leave you. May I personally recommend one book that will get you on the right track in your relationship to Christ. It is the best book available that I know of. The *Liberation of Planet Earth*, by Hal

Lindsey, goes a long way toward explaining the love God has for you. Your new life is just beginning, and we couldn't be happier.

Welcome to eternity.

FOOTNOTES

1. *Altered States of Awareness: Readings From Scientific American* (San Francisco: W.H. Freeman & Co., 1972) pp. 4-14;

2. Blum, p. 189.

3. *FSR*, vol. 12, no. 1, p. 4.

4. FSR, vol. 15, no. 6, pp. 26-28; The Maxwell Cade 5-part series, "A Long Cool Look at Alien Intelligences," vol. 13, no. 4, pp. 14-15; vol. 13, no. 6, pp. 13-15; vol. 14, no. 2, etc. See "Crypto-Sensory Response," FSR Vol. 15., no. 5.

5. From the text of the Stanford Research Institute Film on Uri Geller; Puharich, *Uri* (Bantam Edition), Appendix 2, p. 234; Puharich, *Uri* (Anchor Edition), pp. 216, 269.

6. *FSR*, vol. 16, no. 5, "Phosphenes" article by Bernard E. Finch, M.R.C.S., L.R.C.P., D.Ch., F.B.I.S., pp. 9-10.

7. *FSR*, vol. 8, no. 4, p.7, "Something More Than Science," by Trevor James; vol. 15, no. 6, pp. 23-39, "Thinking Aloud," by Charles Bowen; vol. 15, no. 4, p. 31; no. 5, pp. 31-32; Keel, p. 127, etc. all present ideas similar to these.

8. A. Puharich. *Uri* (Bantam edition), p. 112.

9. Marjorie Fish, "Betty Hills Star Map and Exobiology." Proceedings of the *5th APRO UFO Symposium*, June 15, 1974, pp. 1-8; Blum, pp. 209-219.

10. Ibid.

11. *5th APRO Proceedings*, p. i.

12. Personal correspondence with Dr. David Sanders, University of Chicago, and *National Enquirer*, Sept. 27, 1974.

13. McCall and Levitt, *Satan in the Sanctuary* (Moody Press, 1974.)

14. Shelia Ostrander, Psychic Discoveries Behind the Iron Curtain (Bantam, 1971) p. 99.

15. *Flying Saucers*, pp. 15-16, 33.

Appendix I:

Are the UFO Occupants Good Beings?

If demons are behind the UFO phenomena, we could expect indications of hostility and antichristian theology to come forth. Most of all, we could expect evidence of deception. Satan was called a liar and murderer from the beginning—but also an angel of light, one who could imitate good to accomplish evil ends (John 8:44; 2 Corinthians 11:14). In light of this it is easy to see why demons often appear as friendly spirits to those occultists they communicate with. In the same way, most of those who claim contact with UFO creatures report they are friendly and concerned about the welfare of humanity. This is the perfect deception—evil beings masquerading as benevolent, yet they are not benevolent. The UFO literature is full of indications that UFO entities are evil, hostile beings of great cunning and ability.

Major Donald E. Keyhoe and others have listed many incidents where UFO's have deliberately attached aircraft and been responsible for several deaths and injuries.[1]

In one amazing case in 1953, a F-89 interceptor was scrambled at Kinross AFB to investigate a UFO. The jet followed the UFO over Lake Superior. Then the ground radar control watched amazed as the UFO *merged* with the F-89 on the radar scope! The jet interceptor and the UFO were locked together. The combined blip then moved off the scope, but no trace was ever found of the two pilots, the jet or the UFO. Another incident involved an Air Force C-118 transport plane which was hit by some object in the air. The plane crashed, killing the pilot and the 3 man crew. Prior to the crash, witnesses had seen two UFO's following the aircraft and other people had noted UFO's in the area. Some of the reports were confirmed by Fred Emard, Chief of Police at Orting, Washington. In another case Col. Lee Merkel crashed and was killed just after reporting a UFO. Other cases have undoubtedly been kept secret.

146

The foremost Russian authority on UFO's, Dr. Felix Zigel, of the Moscow Institute of Aviation, has stated that UFO's may have "frightened, harrassed and possibly even killed Russian cosmonauts on their missions."[2] According to some reports, UFO's have simply destroyed planes pursuing them. Books such as Brad Steiger's *Flying Saucers Are Hostile* and Harold Wilkins *Flying Saucers On the Attack* prove at least some of the UFO's are evil. Steiger mentions an entire African village that was destroyed by a UFO beam. Jerome Clark, a leading American UFO researcher, in his article "Why UFO's Are Hostile" mentions the possibility of "hundreds, possibly thousands" of people being murdered around the world by UFO's.[3] Referring to Steiger's book, he says UFO's or their occupants have been responsible for aggravated assault, burnings by direct ray focus, radiation sickness, murders, abductions, pursuits of cars, assaults on homes, paralysis, cremations, disrupting power sources, etc. Jerome Clark says there is "absolutely no objective evidence", apart from contactee cases, that UFO's are either friendly or from other planets. Several other respected researchers as well have noted UFO hostility.

There are also dangerous physical effects resulting from close association with UFO beings or craft. These include blackouts, blindness, sexual assault, psychological disturbances, shock, skin infections, chronic headaches, convulsive seizures and even cancer.[4] In the case of those who claim personal contact with extraterrestrials (contactees), they have reported being programmed, deceived, and made to look like fools. They have suffered the loss of jobs and experienced family disruptions. Reportedly, there are frequent cases of insanity, particularly paranoid schizophrenia, found among contactees and at times they are commanded to murder others. In one incident, a woman starved herself to death after a 66 day fast instituted by her instructor from Jupiter.

There is a very large number of sudden or mysterious deaths, suicides and nervous breakdowns among UFO investigators. Though there are a fair number of reports of UFO healings (via a light ray) and even an operation by extraterrestrials, these are no different than the psychic-occult healings and psychic surgery performed by demons through human instruments.[5] Invariably the person ends up worse off in one way or another.

The UFO occupants themselves seem to be habitual liars. They often contradict each other and espouse obviously false beliefs, if we are to believe the writings and statements of those who claim contact with them.[6] These include: Saturn's civilizations exist in subtropical paradises; Venus has forests, streams, healthy wheat fields, suburban areas etc; the sun and Mercury are not hot, and Pluto is not cold etc. They have said man will never be permitted to set foot on the moon, and have been ignorant of the earth's diameter and basic planetary physics. They have also espoused racist propaganda, particularly against the Jews; urged LSD and drug use and condoned premarital sex. They have made errors of judgment, knowledge and common sense that are absurd and continually espoused the beliefs of occultism, eastern religions and liberal theology. Seemingly without exception they deny the historic Christian faith. They claim to come from every planet in the solar system and then some.

A classic example of deception is the 2,000 page *Urantia Book*, "authored" by some twenty-three supposed extraterrestrials. A full third is devoted to an unbiblical reinterpretation of the life, nature and death of Christ. It denys nearly every Christian belief and has a number of errors—historical, literary, and scientific.[7] In a matter of hours I was able to list over 100 statements in opposition to Biblical Christianity.

Overall, several researchers believe the ufonauts are lying about their origin (outer space), purpose (helping mankind), and identity (extraterrestrials).[8]

These facts, combined with the failure of UFO's to bring help to our troubled world, which they would be expected to do if they were good, demonstrate the evil origin of these beings and the whole UFO phenomenon.[9] *

FOOTNOTES TO APPENDIX I

1. Donald E. Keyhoe *Aliens From Space* pp. 1-3, 157-176; Harold T. Wilkins, *Flying Saucers Uncensored* pp. 132-144 and *Flying Saucers On The Attack* (New York: Ace Books, 1967) pp. 271, 281-3.

2. McWane, *The New UFO Sightings,* p. 143. See also Ostrander and Schroeder, *Psychic Discoveries Behind the Iron Curtain* pp. 94-101; Mufons *Skylook* no. 87, 89.

3. FSR, vol. 13, no. 6, pp. 18-19.

4. For example, see the 1974 MUFON UFO Symposium, p. 92, and the books by Keel, Steiger, Norman, and Blum. Issues of the *Flying Saucer Review* contain many such examples.

5. See FSR, vol 13, no. 5; vol. 15, no. 5; Blum, pp. 144-151; Pedro McGreggor, *Jesus of the Spirits* (Stein and Day, 1967), ch. 8; and the sections of the writings of Drs. Kurt Koch and Merrill Unger dealing with demonic healing.

6. For examples see Chris Evans, *Cults of Unreason* (Farrar, Strauss and Giroux; 1974), pp. 156-170; Steiger, pp. 69-141; Menger, *From Outer Space,* pp. 56-170; and George Adamsky, *Beyond the Flying Saucer Mystery* (Warren, 1974).

7. The *Urantia Book* (Chicago: The Urantia Foundation, 1955). For examples see pp. 836-875, 1066-1084, 2002-2092.

8. Steiger, pp. 16, 63, 145; Keel, p. 102; FSR, vol. 18, no. 5, p. 19; vol. 15, no. 6, p. 26.

9. There are many cases of landed UFO's with occupants who show no signs of being evil entities. However, *The Humanoids* lists several cases of short encounters where the entities gave contactee-type messages, suggesting a link between the two. Since it would be very difficult to divide the entire UFO phenomena into separate non-related parts, it is reasonable to suppose these encounters are manifestations from the same source, attempting to provide support for the ET theory and at the same time a "cover" to draw in serious researchers. Anyway, we shouldn't expect evil to give itself away—that is hardly logical.

Further documentation for the evil aspect of UFO's: people attacked (a few times murdered), abducted, burned, etc. Vallee, *Passport To Magonia,* pp. 12, 13, 20, 131, 146, 161, and case # 23, 113, 118. 352, 372, 398, 417, 449, 457, 486, 514, 542, 583, 608, 636, 641, 790, 816, 844, 881, 885; *The Humanoids,* pp. 57, 59, 93, 95-7, 103-4, 109, 123, 167-8, 182, 192; Keel, *UFO's Operation Trojan Horse,* pp. 31, 45-6, 220-1, 225, 227, 255, 305, 215-220, 270-1, 273, 298, 301, 199, 244-5, 252, 290. From these three classics of ufology there are at least 300 pages, of 900, on which occult/psychic correlations occur.

Appendix II
The Bible and Life in Outer Space

Does the Bible allow for life on other planets somewhere in the universe? Though God could have created life on other planets, this runs into insurmountable Scriptural problems if such beings are behind UFO phenomena.

First of all, the Bible gives no hint of any such life existing. Genesis 1: 14-18 states that the stars and heavens were created for signs, seasons, days and years, and to give light upon the earth, not as places of habitation. Deuteronomy 4:32 implies that God has no convenants with any other beings in the universe. Psalm 115:16 implies human life is unique to the earth. Nowhere in the Bible are other planets ever mentioned. (The King James term "worlds" in Hebrews 1:2 and elsewhere literally means "ages" in the Greek.)

Secondly, some ufonauts are obviously sinful, since they rape, murder, lie and deceive. Thus they are clearly in need of redemption. Here we run into more problems. Scripture implies that the incarnation of Christ was planned and ordained from eternity past to occur at just the proper time.[2] Having once died for man's sin, He is *never* to die again: His work is finished.[3] However, to die for man's sin it was absolutely necessary for Him to become a man, so He could truly represent mankind.[4]

The extraterrestrial problem is that the only way for God to redeem all these supposed millions of creatures is to incarnate *as one of their kind* (Hebrews 2:17) on each of their planets and then to cause Christ to die over and over again. Christ would have to incarnate as a monster, a dwarf, a pyramid-shaped being, someone with six arms or four legs, etc. since this is how some ufonauts appear. Hebrews 9:25-28 shows this is not possible. Would Christ ever be called the brother of a monster (Hebrews 2:11)? Or would a creature that looks like asparagus ever be called a *son* of God? If Christ must die for billions of other creatures, the

149

most sacrificial act in all history—the incarnation with all its implications—becomes a common thing. What was planned from eternity past is no longer unique. Even Christ Himself, the *God-Man,* is no longer unique. History and all things are no longer summed up in Jesus Christ as the Son of *Man,* the Son of *God* (Ephesians 1:10).

Scripture reveals that Christ will return as a glorified human, the Son of Man.[5] The fact that Christ will remain a Man means other fallen creatures could never be redeemed.

Last of all, we will consider Scriptural indications that UFO's could be demonic. The hypothesis that UFO's are examples of Satanic supernatural deception fits in with their evil character, without raising the above problems. Since Scripture says that in the last times Satan will come upon the world with "all power and signs and false wonders, and with all the deception of wickedness" and that God will allow "wonders in the sky above", a phenomenon like Satanic UFO's could almost be expected as our age draws to a close.[6] Ephesians 2:2 refers to Satan when it speaks of "the prince of the *power* of the *air.*" In the original Greek, the word "power" (*exousia*) is a collective term meaning the whole empire of evil spirits, and the term "air" (*aer*) means physical air in the normal sense. The demonic center of power, according to this verse, is the atmosphere around the earth. If the air is the region of the demons' might, we can easily see the UFO interconnection that could exist. All in all, everything one would expect of spiritual warfare and deception can be found in the UFO phenomena. Scripture says we war against the spiritual forces of wickedness *in the heavenly places*" (Eph. 6:12).

While it is true that other fallen races could be expected to deny Christ (just as fallen men do) we would not expect this to be true in nearly every case. And if there is no way to redeem these creatures, why did God create them? And if they deny Christ because they have never heard of Him, is it conceivable that God would not reveal Himself to the billions of races He supposedly created? The more you think on it, the more you understand UFO's for who they are.

The theory that UFO's are of Satanic origin fits in so well with Scripture that it is far and away preferable to a view that sinful, bizarre appearing, but incredibly advanced creatures of God have come across the vast reaches of the universe for unknown reasons to observe or terrorize our planet in such strange ways.

The Bible and Flying Saucers

There appears to be a growing interest in this topic. There are at least fifteen books out attempting to interrelate the Bible and flying saucers, and more are "being rushed to print."[7] Usually these books say that all the miracles of the Bible were done by the intermediacy of UFO's and that Biblical angels are really extraterrestrials. Two of the more popular books, R.L. Dione's *God Drives a Flying Saucer* and Dr. Barry Downing's *The Bible and Flying Saucers* take this position. Saucer theologians however, are invariably poor on scholarship. This includes even the scholarly atempts (e.g. Joseph Blumrich's *The Spaceships of Ezekiel*). They are inconsistent, violate accepted methods of interpretation, ignore contextual considerations, disregard cultural and historical matters, delete or amend the text to support their views, believe the Bible is unreliable or mythological, etc. In reviewing fifteen of these books, Dr. Robert S. Elwood of the University of Southern California concludes they are a "hopeless mass of woolly theories and garbled facts" by authors who were obviously ignorant of the language and cultures of ancient books.[8] However, it is clear that yet another effect of the UFO phenomenon is becoming evident: a reinterpretation of Christianity and the Bible in light of the UFO phenomenon. The Bible is being reinterpreted to be little more than a layman's guide to extraterrestrial visitation of the past. Needless to say, saucer theologians do their readers a great disservice in implying the Bible is related to UFO's. The evidence clearly says otherwise.

FOOTNOTES TO APPENDIX II
1. John 3:16, 18; 17:5.
2. Acts 2:32; Galations 4:4.
3. Romans 6:9; Hebrews 9:22–10:4; 10:12.
4. Philippians 2:5-8; Hebrews 2:17-18; 4:15.
5. Matthew 24:37.
6. 2 Thessalonians 2:9-11; Acts 21:19; Luke 21:11.
7. *Los Angeles Times,* Sept. 8, 1974.
8. APRO Bulletin, September-October 1971.

Appendix III
The Popular Theory on UFO's: A Valid Option?

Though the idea of an outer space origin for UFO's is increasingly popular, their very behavior raises insurmountable problems for such a theory. A few of these problems are listed below.

1. Radar has never recorded the actual entering of UFO's into our atmosphere.[1]

2. If there are thousands of different civilizations "out there," how did they all simultaneously coordinate their efforts to get here at the same time from such widely diverse points in the universe? Why all the interest in our earth, just one little plane? It has been stated that even with one million advanced civilizations, it would be nearly impossible if just *once* a year an actual extra-terrestrial craft were to find us out here on the limb of our galaxy. Yet we are seeing tens of thousands of craft yearly. What chance is there that they would all find our planet, let alone all find it at the same time, let alone all agree to abstain from open contact with humanity, let alone display meaningless antics, etc?

3. UFO investigators almost without exception express bafflement at the phenomena. They don't pretend to have the answers. No accepted theory is capable of explaining all UFO phenomena, except the demonic theory. Several top level UFO researchers have abandoned the extraterrestrial hypothesis (Hynek, Keel, etc.) stating it is no longer a valid alternative for the phenomenon we are experiencing.

4. The aliens seem able to live in our atmosphere without the help of any respiratory devices. Judging from their appearance and supposed diversity of origin, this is extremely hard to explain.

5. They are deliberately secretive, yet one doesn't normally fly trillions of miles to a destination, and then just fly around and go home. Is it not odd that *none* of these civilizations have ever revealed themselves openly? The UFO's disappear upon pursuit, take evasive measures whenever necessary to prevent contact and never openly allow their craft to be

inspected. Despite over 3,000 UFO chases, nothing has been gained.[2] Is this why they came billions of miles? To play hide and seek? Why do such advanced creatures come here often to perform such meaningless antics as buzzing cars, frightening people, or even telling someone a friend has just died? Would they span the galaxies just for this?

6. UFO's have been fired upon hundreds, possibly thousands of times by American, Canadian and Russian pilots, but they have never been able to physically bring one down or capture it.[3]

7. There are a variety of UFO "repair" reports.[4] Are we to believe that craft which can span millions of light years and can literally do unbelievable aeronautic feats, must also be routinely repaired? Are they so poorly constructed that they are no better off than vastly primitive twentieth-century aircraft? And if so, then why have there never been any UFO crashes?

8. The reported dream-like quality of many UFO occupant encounters suggests the event is not real (but probably induced from without).

9. Some very respected researchers have even put forth theories on UFO's that support a demonic hypothesis, such as Dr. Jung, John Keel and others. M.K. Jessup theorized that saucers originate from, and are permanent inhabitants of, the space immediately surrounding the earth.[5] Given the evidence, he said this is more probable than the idea of interstellar craft visting us. Similarily, the whole UFO phenomenon has striking parallels to the powers and abilities demonstrated by the Biblical demons. Sanderson thinks it likely UFO's originate "on or near our own planet".[7]

10. The phenomena of the craft itself-changing shape, size, color, etc. The non-physical aspects are very problematic (merging, splitting, etc.) UFO's have even been reported tipped on end and sticking into the ground or a rock![6] No two UFO's appear exactly alike, implying other civilizations must build and use their craft only once, which would be incredible. Last of all, there has been a recent tremendous upsurge in global UFO activity. Why should this happen at all? There is no satisfactory answer to this question, assuming interstellar visitation. A demonic theory, however, in light of Biblical eschatology, provides a rather concrete explanation.

In conclusion, the statistical considerations against life in outer space (Appendix IV), the characteristics of the UFO phenomenon itself, the high occult correlation and strong parallel to demonic powers, as well as Christian eschatological thought all mitigate against the extraterrestrial theory. Conversely, they all support a demonic theory.

FOOTNOTES TO APPENDIX III

1. *Flying Saucer Review,* vol. 20, no. 2.

2. Donald Keyhoe, *Aliens from Space,* p. 242.

3. Ibid, pp. 1, 42-43.

4. Charles Bowen, ed., *The Humanoids,* p. 39; FSR, vol. 20, no. 2., p. 24.

5. M. K. Jessup, *The Expanding Case For The UFO* (New York: Citadel Press, 1957), pp. 16-17.

6. Gordon Creighton, "The Villa Santina Case," *The Humanoids,* p. 193, note.

7. Ivan Sanderson, *Uninvited Visitors* (New York: Cowles) 1967, p. 176.

Appendix IV

Life by Chance in Outer Space: Possible or Impossible?

It is rapidly becoming almost a dogma among some scientists that since life started by chance on earth and evolved into what we now have, the same must have happened elsewhere. But the chances of this are so remote that they are beyond possibility. Unfortunately, though scientific calculations show more clearly than ever that life could not start any time or any place by chance, scientists are generally unwilling to accept the conclusions these calculations present.

In the October 1969 issue of *Nature* magazine, Dr. Frank Salisbury of Utah State University, currently on leave at the Division of Biomedical and Environment Research at the U.S. Atomic Energy Commission, examined the chance of one of the most basic chemical reactions for the continuation of life taking place. This reaction involves the formation of a specific DNA molecule. It is important to realize that Dr. Salisbury was assuming that life *already* existed. His calculations do not refer to the chance of the *origin* of life from dead matter—something infinitely more improbable—but to the continuance of life already existing.

He calculated the chance of this molecule evolving on 10^{20} hospitable planets, or one hundred, thousand, million, billion planets. This is a figure with twenty zeros after it, and is at least 1,000 times *more* hospitable planets than the number many scientists have estimated could exist. Dr. Salisbury allows four billion years for the chance coming into existence of this molecule on all these planets. But remember he is not speaking here of life as we know it—developed, intelligent living beings, or even of *one* single cell for that matter. He is only calculating the chance of this one appropriate DNA molecule.

He concluded that the chances of just this one tiny DNA molecule coming into existence over four billion years, with conditions just right, on just one of these almost infinite number of

154

hospitable planets, including the earth, as *one chance* in 10^{415}. This is a number with 415 zeros after it. Such a large number is unimaginable, as we will see. Here is how 10^{415} looks in print: 10,000 (thousand) 000 (million) 000 (billion) 000 (trillion) 000 (quadrillion), 000. Even if we packed the entire universe with hospitable planets, so no space was left between them, the chance of this molecule forming on all these planets would still be *one* chance in a figure with 377 zeros after it.[1] This shows that life simply could not originate in outer space, period. But, you ask, isn't there still *one* chance in a number this size, even if it is so large? Given enough time, wouldn't eventually *anything* happen?

Dr. Emile Borel, one of the world's great experts on mathematical probability, formulated a basic law of probability. It states that the occurrence of any event where the chances are beyond one in 10^{50} —a much smaller figure than what we have been dealing with—is an event which we can state with certainty will *never* happen—no matter how much time is alloted, no matter how many conceivable opportunities could exist for the event to take place.[2] In other words, life by chance is mathematically impossible on earth or any place else.*

A rather humorous example will help us to understand the size of very large numbers. Suppose that an amoeba, that microscopic little creature, were given the job of moving the entire universe—the earth, the solar system, all the stars, all the galaxies etc., *one atom* at a time. He had to carry each atom across the entire universe, a distance of thirty billion light years (A light year is the distance light travels in a year going at the speed of 186,000 miles per second). To top it off, he had to carry these atoms at the incredibly slow traveling speed of one *inch* every 15 *billion* years. If this amoeba, traveling one inch in 15 billion years over such a vast distance, moved atom by atom not just one universe, but six hundred thousand trillion trillion trillion trillion universes the size of ours, the number of years it would take him would be "only" 10^{171} years.[3] This is almost infinitely smaller than 10^{415}, the chance that for all practical purposes the universe could evolve one appropriate DNA molecule necessary for a certain chemical reaction!

If you want a *really* big number, try calculating the chance of life *itself* evolving on just one planet, i.e., the earth. Dr. Carl Sagan of Cornell University estimated this to be roughly one chance in ten followed by two *billion* zeros.[4] A number this large would fill over 6,000 books this size just to write it out. A number this size is so infinitely beyond 10^{50} (Borels upper limit for an event to occur) it is simply mind-boggling.

As scientists have faced the logical conclusions of their own research and theories, they have been slow to accept the implications. Dr. George Wald, Nobel prize-winning biologist of Harvard University, stated several years ago: "One only has to contemplate the magnitude of this task to concede that the spontaneous generation of a living organism is impossible. Yet here we are—as a result I believe, of spontaneous generation."[5] This statement might cause us to wonder about the rational thinking of so great a scientist. But a year earlier Dr. Wald stated what evidently was the real problem: "The reasonable view was to believe in spontaneous generation; the only alternative, to believe in a single, primary act of supernatural creation. There is no third position. For this reason many scientists a century ago chose to regard the belief in spontaneous generation as a philosophical necessity.... Most modern biologists, having viewed with satisfaction the downfall of the spontaneous generation hypothesis, yet unwilling to accept the alternative belief in special creation, are left with nothing."[6] And the outstanding biologist D.H. Watson once stated, "If so, it will present a parallel to the theory of evolution itself, a theory universally accepted not because the it can be proved by logically coherent evidence to be true, but because the only alternative, special creation, is clearly incredible."[7] In other words, if I face the alternative of believing a scientific impossibility or believing in the more sensible alternative of a supernatural creator, as a good, rational scientist, I choose to believe in a scientific impossibility! Dr. Cooppedge has an interesting summation for us: "The margin by which chance fails is so vast that no conceivable amount of new discovery along this line could change the basic conclusion that complicated working systems do not arise by chance."[8]

The scientific community has, apparently, never adequately answered Salisbury's article, even though he issued a call for them to solve the dilemma he encountered. In fact, in the five years since the article appeared, there has even been little discussion of it, apparently because its conclusions and implications are too unsettling or embarassing.

It is interesting to note, however, that Salisbury himself has an interest in UFO's and may be willing to concede that extraterrestrials might exist.[9] This does not mean his calculations are wrong. Dr. James F. Coppedge, Director, Probability Research In Biology, was kind enough to check them for me and he declared them quite sound. That Dr. Salisbury shows an interest in the whole extraterrestrial idea is a good example of the attitude expressed by Dr. Wald when he agreed the spontaneous generation of life was impossible, but believed it, because, after all, "here we are." Since man does exist, spontaneous generation must have occurred. And after all, since the UFO's are here, life must exist in outer space. We see that even though Dr. Salisbury's calculations show that life could not exist in outer space, he still thinks UFO's might be real— because after all, here they are! That even some scientists will believe in the impossible only goes to show they are setting up themselves, as well as others, for what might ultimately be the greatest mass deception ever.

Recently, the eminent Nobel prize winner, Dr. Francis Crick, theorized that life on earth might have originated from a spore of life planted long ago by some outer space civilization. This type of reasoning is due mostly to the fact that some scientists are having increasing difficulties believing that life could arise by chance. If however, life was planted here, this supposedly solves the problem. In reality it doesn't solve anything—it just pushes the question back a notch. Where did the life that created us then come from? At some point in the past, life had to have originated by chance, and then we are back where we started with our original question—where did life come from? There is one question, however that is answered by this type of reasoning. It shows how far even brilliant men will go to escape the idea of God being their Creator. It is a sad commentary on the human condition when we find a belief in the obvious replaced by a belief in the impossible. Clearly, God Himself has no second thoughts:

> "It is I who made the earth, and created man upon it. I stretched out the heavens with my hands, and I ordained all their host" (Isaiah 45:2).

FOOTNOTES TO APPENDIX IV

1. 10^{58} planets would pack the universe with earth-size planets. *Elsewhere, Borel uses a figure of 10^{200} in calculations relating to the sciences, however 10^{200} is a very *extreme* concession. The figure of 10^{50}, which Borel himself uses, is more reasonable. Even if we used the 10^{200} figure, however, this would change nothing.

2. Emile Borel, *Probabilities and Life* (New York: Dover, 1962), chapters one and three.

3. James Coppedge, *Evolution: Possible or Impossible* (Grand Rapids: Zondervan, 1974), pp. 118-120.

4. Carl Sagan, ed., *Communication With Extra-Terrestrial Intelligence* (MIT Press, 1973), p. 46.

5. Taken from Henry Morris and John Whitcomb in *The Genesis Flood* (Nutley: Presbyterian and Reformed, 1971), p. 234.

6. Taken from R. Clyde McCone, "Three Levels of Anthropological Objection to Evolution" in the *Creation Research Society Quarterly,* March 1973, p. 208. Used by permission.

7. Taken from Henry Morris, ed., *Scientific Creationism* (San Diego: Institute for Creation Research, 1974), p. 8.

8. Coppedge, p. 113.

9. *Proceedings of the 5th APRO UFO Symposium,* p. 22.

Appendix V
Methods

It is significant that phenomena within the occult world, though from a spiritual "non-material" source, are manifested on the *physical* level. Thus, the "extra-terrestrials" working through Geller can produce 25 tons of force[1] and the spirits who help the Dieri tribe can beach whales for their food.[2] Angels can materialize as humans, speak our language and eat our food.[3] Demons are known to produce just about any conceivable effect on the physical level. They can stop bulldozers, hew down trees and control the weather.[4] The following statement by Dr. Carl Jung is especially relevant here. "For a decade the physical reality of UFOs remained a problematical matter, which was not decided one way or the other with the necessary clarity, despite the mass of observational material that had accumulated in the meantime. The longer the uncertainty lasted, the greater became the probability that this obviously complicated phenomenon had an extremely important psychic component as well as a possible physical basis."[5] He then wonders if UFOs are "something psychic that is equipped with certain physical properties," which is a good statement of demonic abilities. Another strange aspect of UFOs are the apparent "crashes." This includes UFOs disintegrating into a shower of glowing particles or silently "blowing up" with a quick flash of light, and for no apparent reason.[6] In one unverified case a surface-to-air missile totally destroyed a UFO hovering 4 miles above a Navy vessel—no debris was found. Since debris is rarely if ever found, one questions if the UFOs really "explode". This seems rather similar to the UFO repair sightings some people observe where the aliens are outside the landed UFO "repairing" it. Both the "crashes" and the "repairs" seem to be staged events for the viewers benefit. They want them to be observed. That is, they stage these incidents because it's sort of what we would expect from physical craft from other worlds. To help us believe they are physical, they show us "physical" manifestations. Yet are we *really* to believe that with all their demonstrated abilities—instant appearing and disappearing, vastly superior power and manoeuverability etc.—they could really be shot down, or would need regular repairs like our primitive craft?

It appears that the deeper the brain levels, the more open a person is to outside manipulation. For example, most people function at the beta brain wave level during active consciousness. Below this level is the alpha level and then the theta level below that. The farther down you go, the deeper you go into your mind. Reincarnation experiences can be found or induced at the theta levels. (The tool of hypnosis is generally used to "bring out" reincarnation episodes as well as many "forgotten" UFO encounters.)

From this we may theorize that it is the sustained alpha, theta, etc., states which are open to demonic intrusion and this is a possible avenue used to induce certain UFO experiences. Just as Dr. Puharich was *certain* he experienced a series of events, which never really happened, so others are certain they experienced reincarnation episodes (usually done via hypnotic regression), astral flight, or trips on a spaceship. The experience is induced and not real. However, we must also point out that some contact with so-called extraterrestrials is probably real since demons have the ability to assume any shape or form they desire—from elves to humans to monsters. One need only compare the literature of demonology with that of UFOlogy to see the connections. Yet we must carry this one step further. In occult literature there are reports of objects being "astrally produced." In Paramahansa Yoganandas autobiography this includes amulets, trees; astral men capable of assuming any form, food and perfumes. The food can be eaten, the perfume smelled, the men grasped and the amulets worn. Yet they seem to appear "out of nothing". They are said to be structurally evanescent i.e., they must eventually disappear from this world. They are supposedly materializations done by rearranging the vibratory structure of certain energies by yogic power, and not done through hypnotically produced sensations (another yoga technique).[7] Thus, it is possible that these objects are either the result of induced experiences and not real, or that they are supernaturally transported objects from one place to another—a common spiritualist-occult ability, (telekinesis). There is a third possibility. These objects could be materializations of restructured matter which was originally in a different form. This could correspond to the above mentioned rearranging of certain energy levels. Brad Steiger, for example, mentions three books which were in existence several years before the manuscript was in completed form or sent to a publisher. Within a few weeks they had vanished.[8]

Thus, there are five possible answers to the UFO phenomena.

1. Some UFO "reports" are supernaturally faked with no external verification. (Uri's photographs, invisible craft appearing only on radar etc.)

2. Some UFO sightings are selectively induced hallucinations. This occurs when only certain people can see them (contactees, psychics, Geller and Puharich etc) possibly as a result of developing psychic powers. An average person would be unable to see them.

3. Some have external verification which is a false view of reality. Anybody would be able to see them. This would include a type of pro-

jection into the atmosphere, or the use of demons' own bodies, or the manipulation and control of energy and/or radiation, or an apparition or even 3-D holograms with mass. They would be produced phenomena having a type of reality, but used for deceptive purposes. Spacecraft would be seen when there really were no spacecraft from other planets.

4. Possibly the ability to produce real objective craft. This would include the manipulation, transformation and re-moulding of matter.

5. True actual craft from other planets. If these beings were unfallen, Christianity would be proven false, as their messages contradict the Bible. The evidence for Christianity rules this out.

Radiation checks may find higher levels in the area. A soil analysis may find changes have been made in the soil. Bushes and grassy areas may be singed or matted out. Residues may be left. UFOs have cast shadows, shaken school buildings and had bullets bounce off them (Passport to Magonia #. 689, 694, 736). Occultism has parallels in all these areas. Demons are clearly capable of exerting great pressure, causing fires, imprinting images on film, producing radiation and residues, etc. However, to one who does not believe in demonic power, it is an impressive array of evidence.

We know that it is not always easy to distinguish between a very real vision (or dream) and reality (See Acts 12:7-11). Dr. Puharich tells of a situation that happened to him and another woman. They each lived through a series of events as real as anything they had ever experienced. But it never, in fact, really happened! They thought they had had a lengthy conversation with Uri, and two women. However, Uri and Sara denied the whole experience completely and the girl Yaffa in fact was never spoken to over the phone, even though Puharich believed he and the others all talked with her. It was not at all mystical. They were in their apartment and it was just as real as if it really happened. Puharich was badly shaken by the experience. He realized that the whole sequence of events had been imprinted on his minds by the ETs. He came to the conclusion that, given the existence of the ETs he could *never* again know which of his experiences were real and which were not. In fact the space intelligence admitted to Puharich that they could control "almost every thing" that goes on in his head. These are his own words: "These two days' events numbed me. Sarah and Uri experienced one sequence, and Ila and I experienced another in the same time frame. I had discovered the truth about Uri's deepest secret, had had a gun in my hand that felt real, and had had a phone call experience that is real in my mind to this day. But most of all I realized that the four of us had had an experience imprinted on our minds by what could only be the agency of IS. I finally learned that given the existence of IS, I could never again know which of my experiences were directly imposed upon me by IS and which were not.

I have never been so deeply shaken in my life as when I realized the full implication of this power of IS."[9] Now, if these "space beings" can implant a whole series of experiences that never in fact occurred, they can do the exact same in UFO abductions, past lives experiences (reincarnation) and astral projection. Many occult groups are involved in strange experiences that in fact never occur. Paul Twitchell, the founder of Eckankar has "visited" many different "levels of existence" in the cosmos, each with different rulers and inhabitants.[10] The Mighty I-AM founder has had experiences of living for days in underground quarters that contain "houses" similar to plush resorts. They are awakened in the morning by beautiful chiming bells to have classes from the occult "Masters."[11] Howard Menger and hundreds of contactees like him have visited other planets, and seen their landscapes, cities, inhabitants etc.[12] Often during these experiences the contactees or occultists report eating exotic and delicious foods, drinking golden nectar, taking uniquely invigorating showers, communicating with other inhabitants etc. They are all convinced beyond a doubt that their experience was real. In considering all this we now have an explanation for the "terrestrial UFO bases" that some 50 to 100 contactees claim to have visisted. Some say they have been inside of them under the ocean, but this too is just a manipulation of reality.[13] Uri Geller once disappeared into "another dimension" and was gone for at least an hour as far as he could tell. In fact it was only 2 or 3 seconds and his body never disappeared at all. He had two friends with him at the time who said he was never gone. It was a different story to Uri. "This was real—it was all so real—It was so real—so real," he kept saying.[14, 15]

This shows beyond a doubt that a whole range of experiences can be implanted into the minds of those involved in UFOs, the occult or those with psychic abilities. Any medium will tell you her spirit control can interject thoughts or experiences into her mind. Jesus may have had a similar experience, though probably a projection (Luke 4:5—this is not literally possible). Hypnosis is a common method used in UFO investigation. Its usual function is to cause a contactee to relive forgotten UFO experiences. One researcher feels that hypnosis is possibly the next level of standard UFO investigation. Personally I feel that in some of the cases, amnesia and nightmares may have been induced by the "UFO beings" for the express purpose to cause hypnotic methods to be utilized. For some reason, contactees are excellent hypnotic subjects. The first time, they generally go into deep trance and stay there.[16] This is not the normal human experience. For some reason demons can function much better in an altered state of consciousness—be it trance states, drug states, meditation states or hypnotic states. Also several cases of UFO contact appear during the sleeping state wherein the person is awakened. At least he thinks he is. After awakening, the contactee has a variety of experiences with the UFO beings. Later, after the experience is over, he finds himself where he was originally wakened. Sometimes he may be teleported to another place. In cases like these there is nothing to indicate the whole UFO experience was at all real. It could have been implanted in the mind during the sleeping state. The whole idea of "dream feeding" is common in occultism, except a person has experiences with "the spirits" instead of "extraterrestrials."[17]

Further Occult Correlations

1. Strange noises, evolutionary beliefs, sexual intercourse with humans, reincarnation teachings, supernatural knowledge of languages, cultural adaptations, psychic healing, possession ability, a training period for the contacted person, etc., are common to both the spirits of occultism and the aliens of ufology.

2. Much of black magic and witchcraft have a strong link to astrology.[18] For example, certain magic rituals involve a belief that each of the planets of the zodiac have a corresponding spirit. There is a warning in the Kabbalistic Master Ritual that planetary forms can perform tricks on the initiate, one of which is posing as the most sexually desirable person imaginable.[19] This is similar to the Villas Boas case where he was abducted by UFO beings and then seduced by a female extraterrestrial who had the most beautiful body he had ever seen.[20] The Rosicrucians, Theosophical "Masters" and the Hermetic Order of the Golden Dawn (related to Hitler's movement) all were involved with the highest category of magic ritual. This involves communication with immensely powerful astral entities known as "Group Forms" who have the ability to take human shape.[21] This is reminiscent of humanoid UFO occupants.

3. Paul Twitchell, founder of the admittedly dangerous occult system of Eckankar admits to conversing astrally with a being from Venus who espoused the teachings of Eckankar.[22] He notes the tie-in to occultism and the extraterrestrial's teachings.[23] Twitchell says UFOs are not from outer space but are "perfectly natural astral projections of the psychic world" and that occult adepts commonly witness UFOs in their astral (out of the body) travels.[24] In other words UFOs are the projections of astral beings from the astral sphere. (This is not much different from a demonic hypothesis).

4. The Kabbalistic Master Ritual includes the following effects: loss of the normal state of reason, violent psychic assaults against the practitioner, poltergeist manifestations, exhaustion after the entities departure, possessions and also warnings of death. All these reports parallel various UFO reports.[25]

5. The volume *Breakthrough: An Amazing Experiment in Electronic Communication with the Dead* (K. Raudive, 1971) is an account of the spirits of the "dead" (i.e. demons) who have imprinted voices on magnetic tape, over 70,000 times, (up to six different languages in one sentence). Besides the material being unbiblical, it is all very reminescent of Geller's extra-terrestrials imprinting their voices on cassette tapes.

6. Both Jacques Vallee and John Keel point out the bizarre parallels between the hundreds of reports of occultists sexual intercourse with demons on one hand and the similar reports of sexual intercourse with extraterrestrials on the other. Keel says the UFO occupant's sexual encounters essentially "follow the patterns of the well known incubus-succubus phenomenon found in religious and psychic lore."[26]

7. We find in occultism that initial contact with the spirit starts a process of heightening psychic powers, which if continued reaches a peak level. Similarily there are many cases of persons reportedly hit by a UFO beam who trace their newly developed psychic abilities to that event, and their powers grow as they continue contact. In both cases, this "mystical illumination" may sooner or later culminate in possession by a foreign entity, whether spirit guide or extraterrestrial. Also, in many UFO reports involving a close encounter, even where there was no occupant sighting, the observer notices some type of mental control being exerted over him, described as similar to being "charmed" or hypnotized. The parallel to mediumship, wherein the demon induces a trance state in the person is obvious.[27]

8. Just as contact with spirits of the occult results in a variety of

harmful effects, contactees involvement with the space entities result in similar maladies. (see, Kurt Koch and John Keels books.) There are also parallels in geographical preference for UFOs and demons (eg Brazil).

9. Medium Estelle Roberts included a photograph of Red Cloud, her spirit guide in her autobiography, *Fifty Years A Medium.* He looked just like a Indian Chieftan complete with headdress—showing a demonic ability to assume probably any form imaginable—from gnomes to UFOs to aliens from space. Keel states: "On the one hand, all the real facts of the situation, the manifestations and physical effects of the phenomenon, seem to point to a negative, paraphysical explanation. The UFOs do not seem to exist as tangible manufactured objects. They do not conform to the accepted natural laws of our environment. They seem to be nothing more than transmogrifications tailoring themselves to our abilities to understand. The thousands of contacts with the entities indicate that they are liars and put on artists. The UFO manifestation seem to be, by and large, merely minor variations of the age-old demonological phenomenon." (Operation Trojan Horse p. 299)

10. Bryant and Helen Reeve spent two years interviewing contactees around the world. In nearly every case where communication was established it was by occult methods. These included projections of consciousness, automatic writing, (implanted thought) dictation, emergence, ESP, telepathy, clairaudience, clairvoyance, mediumship, samadhic (yogic) meditation the akashic records, sound and sight rays, etc. The space beings strongly urge a movement into occultism if man is to progress. (Flying Saucer Pilgrimage, ch 26, 27)

11. The demonic hypothesis depends largely on the occult—psychic interrelation of UFO reports as well as the alien's reported denial of Biblical truth. The following material in the Flying Saucer Review (by volume and number) is included because it is recognized as a standard UFO information source and known for its reliability in research and reporting. Dr. Vallee says it is a publication "specializing in high quality documentation of UFO phenomena", and Dr. J. Allen Hynek says it is "the best UFO magazine in the world. The listings are far from exhaustive. Volume 16 # 5 p. 25 Theorizes that UFO contactee cases could result from imposed hallucinations. "Many accounts by contactees are permeated by a definite dream-like quality which, in addition to anomalies of "time-lapse" or "time-gain", are comparable to para-psychological events experienced by practising occultists."/18 # 6, p. 25-7 telepathy, interjection of thoughts/11 # 6, p. 19-21 Correlation to UFO incidents and the myths, legends and folktales of primitive people—several tribes listed; magic powers, sorcery, prophecies/11 # 4, p. 24 Abduction; a recommendation is made that all the records of psychism, demonology, witchcraft and related areas should be re-considered in the light of UFO phenomena now occurring; possible Incubi and Succabae, similarity of UFO beings to traditional leprechauns/16 # 5, p. 18-20 reported outbreak of poltergeist activity in UFO flap-areas; it is recognized that UFO literature contains "a great many incidences" closely similar to poltergeist and ESP phenomena; hypnosis, telepathy, UFOs can affect human brains, people hypnotised, paralyzed by UFOs; UFO sounds are reported *directly* in the brain not via the ears; people hypnotised, paralyzed by UFOs; UFOs can produce hallucinations, personality changes, speech alterations, visions, inspirations, psychic phenomena, and possibly an

expanded awareness similar to the effects of LSD and other psychedelic drugs; astral projection, clair-audience, precognition/16 # 5, p. 23-4 materialisation, pungent odor, connection mentioned between UFOs and psychic phenomena, spectre-like UFO occupants, dream-like experiences, suggestion that landed UFOs may be induced illusions, "psychic-type projections" into the mind of observers, suggestion that contactee may be controlled by UFOs for their purposes.

17 # 1, p. 24-27 there is use of the dream state in UFO communication with a medium. A "strange force" dominated his mind. He was "completely paralysed," and a "beam of light" dominated his thoughts, movements, and will power. They claimed to be preparing him for a journey to other planets/17 # 2, p. 32-3 Using the 16th century authority on demonology, *Demonolatry* by Nicholas Remey connections are shown to UFO phenomena. A similarity to the complexity of forms taken by demons and UFO beings, smell of sulphur common to both, similarity in vast knowledge of spoken languages/15 # 2, p. 13-14 contemplates the possibility of hallucinatory type images being imposed on the mind/13 # 4, p. 11-13 Paralyzation, possible astral projection/13 # 4, p. 14-15 mental influence or control by UFO beings/10 # 2, p. 12; 18 # 5 p. 17; Correlation to fairy lore psychic phenomena and many occult manifestations/18 # 4, p. 24—headaches, serious eye impairment/16 # 1, p. 25 sexual assault and "abduction"/16 # 5, p. 23—blindness, paralysis/18 # 3. p. 4—"beams of light that kill or maime."/18 # 4, p. 4—Mentions "well-attested cases" where witnesses have encountered UFOs of sinister character. Also, there was a possible tie in between UFOs and the Aberfan (West Wales) land disaster (144 dead)/9 # 3, pp. 13—shock/12 # , p. 4 headaches, dizziness visual, auditory and olfactory hallucinations, emotional changes, delusions, amnesia with psychotic aspects, epilepsy like discharge with loss of consciousness/18 # 6, p. 25—hospitalization required/11 # 2, p. 14—the death of M. K. Jessup is mentioned as being just one of several mysterious deaths involved in UFO phenomena/15 # 2—Green beam of light struck Inacio de Souza, 41. Headaches, nausea and burns on the first to third days. He developed cancer and died less than two months later. Reports of paresthesia (tingling sensation). (This is reported among mediums and occultists just before going into trance or before the "entity" entering their body.) Temporary paralysis and similar effects are not infrequent among UFO reports, "sleep paralysis" (cataplexy) reported, genitourinary effects also./13 # 6, p. 13-15 Presents possible theories and evidence for possession and mental illness in relationship to some UFO cases/15 # 6, p. 26-8 in considering the whole range of UFO phenomena Mr. Bowen speculates about its "strange dreamlike quality." He says that UFO contact cases could be accounted for by the events being implanted in the mind through hypnosis, radiation or some other means. Possibly he says, the whole experience could be implanted from far away or from another dimension. He says the power could be great enough so that witnesses would inflict wounds upon themselves and imagine physical contact with the entity. Special Issue no. 2 June 1969: a young woman spent a year in a mental institution after approaching a UFO; a policeman experiences terrible headaches, increased IQ, expanded powers of ESP; prophecy by two contactees on weather and earth movements. They were in mental contact

with extraterrestrials and have a very high degree of accuracy; a former Air Force pilot who has communicated with "them" for 4 months says they are "ruthless in pursuit of their objectives."/ 20 # 3, p. 22-3, 27 notes the high correlation of the UFO phenomenon and occult phenomena in many areas.

Listings From Other Sources

Paralysis, blacking out, possession, thousands of cases of amnesia where the person has been involved with psychic phenomena and UFOs. (1, 2, 5)/ Possession, Demonology, black magic, fairy myths, sulphur odors, poltergeist manifestations, chronic headaches, occult in general. (2, 3, 8, 10, 12, 14)/ History of occultism in the family, reincarnation beliefs, encouragment to believe in Edgar Cayce's writings, hypnotic regression succabae, purposeful lies. (12, 13)/ Deception, UFO ignited forest fire, contact with the dead, reincarnation, blinding a man, contact via yoga, medium receiving UFO messages (4, 24, 25)/ Death, unfamiliar language spoken in trance, blinding, paralysis, telepathy (5, 7)/ Automatic writing contact, ouija board contact; Terrible cold chills, severe headaches, sulphur odors, partial loss of consciousness, astral projection (these occurred after the 3rd attempt at contact with extraterrestrials (8, 11)/ Succubae, psychic communication (9)/ Automatic writing, hypnotism used by UFO beings, general occult tie-in, lies, admission of deception, occult history, tingling sensation, coldness; lawyer, gynecologist, scientist, contactees; Meterologist from University of Arizona discusses the possibility that aliens are systematically taking over top positions in government and military: notation that UFO beings are extremely skilled in psychological warfare; Death apparently from UFO ray; "Monster" report (13)/ Psychosis, disappearing black cadillacs (men in black phenomena) strange phone calls, radio-Tv effects, shrinking UFO deposits, telepathy, unusual events, several reports of terrible stenches, monster reports, mutilated animals; a 16 gauge shotgun fired point blank at an alien who just disappeared, etc. (14, 16)/ "Angel Hair", explosion heard when UFO disappeared, unusual mental, physical effects in low level UFO sightings; a feeling of being charmed or hypnotised by the UFO (15)/ Symptoms of radiation poisoning, irresistible sleepiness, nervousness after contact, terrible headaches, buzzing in the head, welts, mind control, paralysis, the mind hurting, etc. (17)/ Paralyzed legs, teleportation, hatha yoga, mediumship, 14 fires started over an 11 day period during a UFO flap, possible heart attacks, brain hemorrhages, death, large scale abductions (?), overpowering stench, shock, red jagged marks on the waist, shoulders, back. (19, 21)/Eastern Occult beliefs, exploding fiery balls, teleportation, reincarnation on another planet (20).

Salvador Freixedos new book *El Diabolics Inconsciente* draws parallels "between the behaviour of UFOs and demons . . . (he) believes that UFOs help us prove the reality of many demonic happenings and that demonology aids us in understanding the possible motives of UFO phenomena." (FSR Vol 20 # 4, p. 28). Finally, John A Keel states: "Are there really thousands of different sizes and shapes flitting around our skies, as the ufologists would like us to believe? Or are most of these objects temporary manipulations of matter and energy? We must now ask if there could not be some validity to a hypothesis that the objects are transmogrifications and we rarely if ever see them in their real form." "In short, "Flying saucers" might not be any more real than the "dirigibles" of 1897 and the "mystery airplanes" of 1934. Their existence as solid, manufactured physical objects cannot be proven. They may be nothing more than transmuted energy patterns coexisting with us in the unseen, indetectable high-frequency radiations which surround us.... The intelligence behind them remains to be defined, just as their real purpose may be incomprehensible to us.[22]

Footnotes (other sources)

(1) Normal, p. 144, 142, 120, 112, 110, 57, 50, 30 (2) Keel p. 198-9, 130, 107, 122 (3) Keel (Operation Trojan Horse) p. 53; on most pages (4) FSR Vol 18 # 5; 14 # 2p34; 16 # 5 p23; 16 # 1 p11 (5) Flammonde, P. *The Age of Flying Saucers* p. 60-65, 189 (7) Edwards, F. *Flying Saucers Serious Business* (1966) p. 115 (8) David, Jay *The Flying Saucer Reader* (New York: Signet 1967) p. 61-94 (9) Cowles and Lipi (eds.) *Flying Saucers* (1968) p. 138, 137, (10) Fuller, *The Interrupted Journey,* P. IX (11) APRO Bulletin Sept./Oct. 1973 p. 4 (12) Steiger P. 23, 50, 58, 25, 71, 146, 149, 36 (13) Sagas UFO Report Spring 1974 p. 37-8; Summer 74 p. 6, 8, 30-31, 50, Sagas UFO Special Vol. 3 p. 29. 37, Saga Magazines June 1974, Sagas UFO Special 1973 p. 46, *Midnight* Oct. 14, 1974, p. 29 Keel p. 130 (14) Mufon 1974 Symposium p. 84-7, 89-91, 92, 133-49 (15) Emenegger p. 94, 96, 109, 155 (16) Puharich, *Uri* (17) Blum p. 180-181, 184, 110-116, (18) Bergier p. 88 (19) McWane p. 111-114, 118-30, 147 (20) Menger, H. p. 54-7, 88, 115, 120, 161 (21) Wilkins p. 53, 84, 82, 116-117, 100-101 (22) FSR Vol 15 # 4, p. 31 (23) Trench, *Mysterious Visitors, The UFO Story* (New York, Stein and Day), 1971 pp. 49-97 (24) David St. Clair *The Psychic World of California* (New York: Bantam) 1973, pp. 316-26; 134-7 (25) Colin Wilson, *The Occult* (New York, ventage) 1973, pp. 527-533.

Footnotes (Methods/Correlations)

1. Blum, p. 255; 2. Rose, Primitive Psychic Power (1968) p. 128; 3. Genesis 19; 4. Twitchell, All About ECK (1973) p. 44, Steiger, In My Soul I Am Free p. 13; 5. Jung, p. 17; 6. Keyhoe, Aliens From Space p. 43-5, 158; 7. Autobiography of a Yogi, p. 54-7, 21-2, 316, 480-1, 475-6; 8. Steiger (above) p. 23-4; 9. Puharich p. 112; 10. Twitchell, The Tigers Fang; 11. King, The Magic Presence, (St. Germain Press, 1969) p. 118-20; 12. Menger, p. 92-5, 144; 13. McWane, p. 118-9, 13; 14. Puharich, p. 179, 212-13 (Anchor); 15. Norman, p. 118; 16. 5th APRO Symposium, p. 17; 17. Brown, The Heyday of Spiritualism, p. 89-91, 1-100, A. J. Davis and the Arabula (1867); 18. Thomas, Religion and the Decline and Fall of Magic, Ch. 21; 19. Conway, p. 120-1; 20. The Humanoids p 216; 21.

Conway, p. 120-1; 22. Twitchell, The Spiritual Notebook p. 64, 125, 70-81, Dialogues with the Master, p. 165-72; 23. TWitchell, Intro. to Eckankar p. 30-31, 46-7; 24. Twitchell, All About ECK, p. 68-70, 25. Conway, Ch 7; 26. Vallee, p. 126-9, Keel p. 160-61; 27. Keel. p. 218-9, Emenegger, p. 94, Keyhoe, p. 11, Gasson. p1-87.